SIGNS AND SECRETS OF THE MESSIAH

A FRESH LOOK AT THE MIRACLES OF JESUS IN THE GOSPEL OF JOHN

BIBLE STUDY GUIDE | FIVE SESSIONS

RABBI JASON SOBEL

WITH **WAYNE HASTINGS**

HarperChristian
Resources

Signs and Secrets of the Messiah Bible Study Guide
© 2023 by Jason Sobel

Requests for information should be addressed to:
HarperChristian Resources, 3900 Sparks Dr. SE, Grand Rapids, Michigan 49546

ISBN 978-0-310-17215-4 (softcover)
ISBN 978-0-310-17216-1 (ebook)

All Scripture quotations, unless otherwise indicated, are from the Tree of Life (TLV) Translation of the Bible. Copyright © 2015 by The Messianic Jewish Family Bible Society.

Scripture quotations marked CJB are taken from the Complete Jewish Bible. Copyright © 1998 by David H. Stern. All rights reserved. No portion of this book may be reproduced, stored in a retrieval system, or transmitted in any form or by any means without prior written permission of the publisher.

Scripture quotations marked ESV are taken from The ESV® Bible (The Holy Bible, English Standard Version®). ESV® Text Edition: 2016. Copyright © 2001 by Crossway, a publishing ministry of Good News Publishers. The ESV® text has been reproduced in cooperation with and by permission of Good News Publishers. Unauthorized reproduction of this publication is prohibited. All rights reserved.

Scripture quotations marked NIV are taken from the Holy Bible, New International Version®, NIV®. Copyright © 1973, 1978, 1984, 2011 by Biblica, Inc.® Used by permission. All rights reserved worldwide. The "NIV" and "New International Version" are trademarks registered in the United States Patent and Trademark Office by Biblica, Inc.®

Scripture quotations marked NKJV are taken from the New King James Version®. Copyright © 1982 by Thomas Nelson. Used by permission. All rights reserved.

Scripture quotations marked NLT are taken from the *Holy Bible*, New Living Translation, copyright © 1996, 2004, 2015 by Tyndale House Foundation. Used by permission of Tyndale House Publishers, Inc., Carol Stream, Illinois 60188. All rights reserved.

Any internet addresses (websites, blogs, etc.) and telephone numbers in this study guide are offered as a resource. They are not intended in any way to be or imply an endorsement by HarperChristian Resources, nor does HarperChristian Resources vouch for the content of these sites and numbers for the life of this study guide.

HarperChristian Resources titles may be purchased in bulk for church, business, fundraising, or ministry use. For information, please e-mail ResourceSpecialist@ChurchSource.com.

First Printing June 2023 / Printed in the United States of America

23 24 25 26 27 LBC 5 4 3 2 1

CONTENTS

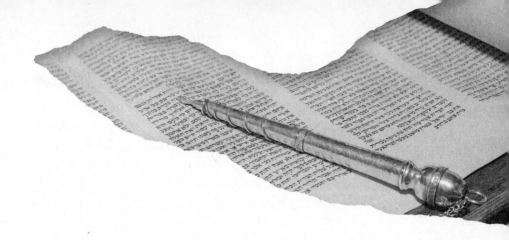

I never have any difficulty
believing in miracles since
I experienced the miracle of a
change in my own heart.

AUGUSTINE OF HIPPO[1]

A NOTE FROM
RABBI JASON SOBEL

I'm always excited to be involved in miracles. Miracles show us that Jesus (His Hebrew name is Yeshua) is alive and working in this world. I've witnessed miracles in my own life and in the lives of others, and I've found that nothing will ignite one's faith like a miracle. If we are Christians, walking in the supernatural should be natural for us—a part of our day-to-day spiritual lives. God has been doing miracles from the beginning of time. He did them in the Old Testament, He did them in the New Testament, and He is still doing them today. It's just part of His character.

In this study, you will be exploring Yeshua's miracles in the Gospel of John in a way that I believe will increase your faith that you can have miracles in your own life. The Bible says that it is the "glory of God to conceal a matter and the glory of kings to search it out" (Proverbs 25:2). So, as a child of the King, you will be immersing yourself in the wonder and mystery of God's Word to uncover His truths. The Bible is like a multifaceted diamond—its many sides contribute to its brilliance. There are many ways to read Bible text that are complementary and never contradictory. It's not worthless but worthwhile to look at every word from many angles.

The Bible is also like the ocean—shallow enough for any child and deep enough that you cannot explore all of it. There are infinite layers to God's Word, which is what makes the Bible different from any other book written by a human author. There is always some new mystery or secret to be uncovered. So, while deeper spiritual truths are often not obvious on the surface, *they can be found*—and it's to the glory of your King to seek them out and meditate on them. The more you look at the languages of the Bible, make connections between the Old and New Testaments, and consider the numeric connections, the more secrets and mysteries (deeper meaning in the Scriptures) will be revealed to you.

As we take this journey, I pray that God will lead you to new insights and breakthroughs and that He will reveal Himself to you with a sense of His presence and shalom.

— Rabbi Jason Sobel

HOW TO USE THIS GUIDE

Welcome to this study on the *Signs and Secrets of the Messiah* as recorded in the Gospel of John. Before you begin, note that there are a few ways you can go through the material. You can experience this study with others in a group (such as a Bible study, Sunday school class, or any other small-group gathering), or you may choose to study the content on your own. Either way, the videos for each session are available for you to view at any time via streaming.

GROUP STUDY

Each session is divided into two parts: (1) a group study section and (2) a personal study section. The group section is intended to provide a basic framework on how to open your time together, get the most out of the video content, and discuss the key ideas that were presented in the teaching. Each session includes the following:

- **Welcome:** A short note about the topic of the session for you to read on your own before you meet together as a group.
- **Connect:** A few icebreaker questions to get you and your group members thinking about the topic and interacting with one another.
- **Watch:** An outline of the key points that will be covered in each video teaching to help you follow along, stay engaged, and take notes.
- **Discuss:** Questions to help your group reflect on the teaching material presented and apply it to your lives.
- **Respond:** A short personal exercise to help reinforce the key ideas.
- **Pray:** A place for you to record prayer requests and praises for the week.

If you are doing this study in a group, make sure you have your own copy of this study guide so you can write down your thoughts, responses, and reflections and have access to the videos via streaming. You will also want to have a copy of the *Signs and Secrets of the Messiah* book, as reading it alongside the curriculum will provide you with deeper insights. (See the notes at the beginning of each group session and personal study section on which chapters of the book you should read before the next group session.) Finally, keep these points in mind:

- **Facilitation:** If you are doing this study in a group, you will want to appoint someone to serve as a facilitator. This person will be responsible for starting the video and keeping track of time during discussions and activities. If *you* have been chosen for this role, there are some resources in the back of this guide that can help you lead your group through the study.

- **Faithfulness:** Your small group is a place where tremendous growth can happen as you reflect on the Bible, ask questions, and learn what God is doing in other people's lives. For this reason, be fully committed and attend each session so you can build trust and rapport with the other members.

- **Friendship:** The goal of any small group is to serve as a place where people can share, learn about God, and build friendships. So seek to make your group a "safe place." Be honest about your thoughts and feelings . . . but also listen carefully to everyone else's thoughts, feelings, and opinions. Keep anything personal that your group members share in confidence so that you can create a community where people can heal, be challenged, and grow spiritually.

If you are studying *Signs and Secrets of the Messiah* on your own, read the opening Welcome section and reflect on the questions in the Connect section. Watch the video and use the outline provided to take notes. Personalize the questions and exercises in the Discuss and Respond sections. Close by recording any requests that you want to pray about during the week.

PERSONAL STUDY

The personal study is for you to experience on your own during the week. Each exercise is designed to help you explore the key ideas you uncovered during your group time and delve into passages of Scripture that will help you apply those principles to your life. Go at your own pace, doing a little each day or all at once, and spend a few moments in silence to listen to what God might be saying to you. Each personal study includes:

- **Open:** A brief introduction to lead you into the personal study for the day.
- **Read:** A few passages on the topic of the day for you to read and review.
- **Reflect:** Questions for you to answer related to the passages you just read.

If you are doing this study as part of a group, and you are unable to finish (or even start) these studies for the week, you should still attend the group time. Be assured that you are still wanted and welcome even if you don't have your "homework" done. The group studies and personal studies are intended to help you hear what God wants you to hear and to apply what He is saying to your life. So be listening for Him to speak as you explore the miracles of Yeshua as recorded in the Gospel of John and how they apply to your life today.

WEEK 1

BEFORE GROUP MEETING	Read chapters 1–2 in *Signs and Secrets of the Messiah* Read the Welcome section (page 3)
GROUP MEETING	Discuss the Connect questions Watch the video teaching for session 1 Discuss the questions that follow as a group Do the closing exercise and pray (pages 3–8)
STUDY 1	Complete the personal study (pages 10–12)
STUDY 2	Complete the personal study (pages 13–15)
STUDY 3	Complete the personal study (pages 16–17)
CONNECT AND DISCUSS	Connect with someone in your group (page 18)
CATCH UP AND READ AHEAD (before week 2 group meeting)	Read chapters 3–4 in *Signs and Secrets of the Messiah* Complete any unfinished personal studies

THE SIGNS AND SECRETS OF TRANSFORMATION

*As the headwaiter tasted the water that had become wine,
he calls the bridegroom and says to him, "Everyone brings out the
good wine first, and whenever they are drunk, then the worse.
But you've reserved the good wine until now!"*

JOHN 2:9–10

Shalom, and welcome to the first session of *Signs and Secrets of the Messiah*. I'm excited to walk with you through the signs, mysteries, and miracles of Yeshua as recorded in John 2.

As the story opens in John's Gospel, we find Yeshua at a wedding. Jewish weddings are incredibly celebratory, and wine is essential to the post-ceremony party. Here, Yeshua performs His first miracle as He turns plain water into finely aged wine. His mother, Mary, plays a significant role in this miracle, as do the servants who fill six large urns with water.

Mary, as she watches the newly married couple, sees what could be an embarrassing situation develop. The couple has run out of wine! She sees the need and asks her Son, Yeshua, for help. Mary speaks boldly to the servants, telling them to "do whatever He tells you" (John 2:5). They respond without question. Mary's boldness, or *chutzpah* in Hebrew, is noteworthy.

Interestingly, in John's Gospel, the first event at which Yeshua reveals His identity is a *wedding*. Why? Because the final event in Revelation is the marriage of the Messiah to His people (see Revelation 19–22). Author Brant Pitre underscores this point: "In later Jewish tradition, it came to be believed that this feast of God would be a kind of return to Eden, in which the righteous would drink *miraculous* wine that had its origins at the very dawn of time."[2] Yeshua is the ultimate bridegroom. He is coming for His bride, serving not ordinary but miraculous wine. John 2 gives us a sneak preview of this ultimate wedding celebration.

CONNECT | 15 MINUTES

If you or any of your group members don't know each other, take a few minutes to introduce yourselves. Then, to get things started, discuss one of these questions:

- What excites you about this study? What do you hope to learn from it?

  — *or* —

- What comes to mind when you think about Yeshua's miracles? Why?

WATCH | 20 MINUTES

Now watch the video for this session, which you can access by playing the DVD or through streaming (see the instructions provided with this guide). Below is an outline of the key points covered during the teaching. Record any thoughts or concepts that stand out to you.

OUTLINE

   I. Messiah's first miracle occurred during a wedding in Cana (see John 2:1–11).

      A. It is significant that Yeshua's changing the water into wine occurred at a Jewish wedding.

      B. God's relationship with His people is often symbolized in Scripture as marriage (see Ezekiel 16:8).

      C. The miracle is a prophetic sign of the coming messianic wedding that we will celebrate with Yeshua, Jesus, our bridegroom, in the messianic Kingdom.

  II. The miracle happened on the third day. Why is this significant?

      A. The third day was the only day in Creation that God blessed twice.

      B. The third day was the day that God revealed Himself on Mount Sinai.

      C. The third day was the day of resurrection.

 III. Yeshua is the greater than Moses. Instead of turning water into blood, He turned water into wine.

      A. Wine symbolizes the abundance, fruitfulness, and blessing of the messianic Kingdom. Yeshua came that we might have life and have it more abundantly (see John 10:10).

      B. There's also significance in the six pots.

         1. 6 in Hebrew is the number of connection.

         2. Yeshua died on a Friday, the 6th day on the Hebrew calendar.

 IV. The miracle didn't occur until the wine ran out.

      A. Oftentimes in our lives, God doesn't move until we've come to the end of a challenge or difficulty.

      B. The eleventh hour should not be one of discouragement but of hope, expectation, and transformation.

      C. God can take the ordinary and transform it into something extraordinary.

  V. Purification is an integral part of transformation (see John 2:12–17).

      A. A purging needs to occur that removes the old to bring in the new.

      B. Yeshua needed to purify the Temple before Passover.

      C. The leaven (or sin) had to be removed from His Father's house.

NOTES

Hosea 2:19+13 Betrothal
Jesus overturns the money changers
in the Temple twice in His ministry.
Once at the beginning + once at
the end.

spiritual lever = sin
Purging

DISCUSS | 35 MINUTES

Take a few minutes to discuss what you just watched by answering these questions.

1. Read Isaiah 25:6; Amos 9:13–14; and John 2:11. Wine was a critical part of a Jewish wedding, as wine—in abundance—symbolized joy and blessed days. How do you think this miracle affected the disciples? How would it have affected you?

2. Scripture talks about God's relationship with His people, and it is often compared to a wedding. Describe how that relationship looks to you. If God is the groom and we are the bride, how should that principle affect our daily walk with Him?

3. What does this first miracle reveal about Yeshua's character, identity, and mission? What does this story reveal about Mary and the servants who fulfilled her instructions?

4. What did you learn about the third day and its double blessing? From where or whom does our double blessing come? How can we increase our relationship with Yeshua to experience the fruitfulness of the double blessing?

5. Ask someone in the group to read aloud John 2:3. Notice that Yeshua's miracle didn't happen until the wine *ran out*. When was a time in your life that you experienced God showing up just when you thought, *The wine has run out!*

RESPOND | 10 MINUTES

Yeshua's first miracle happened in response to His mother's, Mary's, request, and she didn't take no for an answer! Running out of wine was a major social mistake and could have impacted the couple's standing in the community for a long time. But Mary fully *expected* her Son to do something. She had faith, trust, and *chutzpah*—holy boldness and audacity.

> On the third day, there was a wedding at Cana in the Galilee. Yeshua's mother was there, and Yeshua and His disciples were also invited to the wedding. When the wine ran out, Yeshua's mother said to Him, "They don't have any wine!" Yeshua said to her, "Woman, what does this have to do with you and Me? My hour hasn't come yet." His mother said to the servants, "Do whatever He tells you."
>
> John 2:1-5

Chutzpah is having the faith to stand firm or boldly when necessary, move forward, and take big risks for God when led. Mary stood boldly and wouldn't take no for an answer when she talked to Jesus at the wedding in Cana. She was willing to risk everything because of her faith. Faith, in many ways, is spelled R-I-S-K. Having faith will embolden us to take risks.

What is your understanding of "holy boldness" or *chutzpah* in your life?

How do you regain your holy boldness during those times your faith seems weak?

PRAY | 10 MINUTES

Spending time together in your small group is important. So set aside some time after each session for group prayer. You can set boundaries so your group remains focused on each other's needs and concerns, or set a time limit, as some people can be distracted by their need to pick up children or different personal needs. Remember, some people have never prayed aloud or in front of others, so help everyone feel accepted and warmly invite them to pray. Also, try to spend some time focused on the session's lesson. Some prayer times can stray from the lesson, so be aware and keep the time focused. Finally, write down the prayer requests so group members can pray for their brothers and sisters throughout the week.

Name	Request

PERSONAL STUDY

One of the most important ways to learn more about God and all He has for us is to study His Word and dig deeper into what He is telling us. These personal studies aim to help you reflect and grow spiritually by applying more of the truth of God's Word in your life. As you work through each day's study, write down your responses to the questions, as you will be given a few minutes to share your insights at the start of the next session (if you are doing this study with others). If you are reading *Signs and Secrets of the Messiah* while doing this study, first read the book's introduction and chapters 1 and 2.

LIFE OVER DEATH

In this week's group time, we discussed Jesus' miracle of turning water into wine at a wedding in Cana. In many ways, Jesus transforming the water into wine is like the miracle of Moses turning the Nile River into blood during the ten plagues (see Exodus 7:20).

Moses' first miracle when he delivered Israel from Egypt was turning the Egyptians' most critical source of water and agriculture, the Nile, into blood. When you think about it, that's like stopping all our water supplies used for drinking and irrigating. Jewish sages offer many explanations as to why the first plague brought upon the Egyptians was *dam* (Hebrew for "blood"). The Nile made Egypt a very fertile and prosperous nation. Since the Nile was the source of their sustenance, the Egyptians worshiped it as a deity. They personified the Nile as the god *Hapi*, to whom they offered sacrifices. The Egyptians also believed that Pharaoh, the god incarnate, was responsible for controlling and maintaining nature's harmony.

Another reason for the plague of turning the Nile into blood was to punish the Egyptians, who had shed the blood of defenseless Jewish children (see Exodus 1:22). Thus, the blood of the innocent babies cried out for justice from the depths of the Nile and bore witness against Egypt. This plague was particularly fitting, for it follows the principle of *mida keneged mida* (measure for measure). Based on both explanations, we learn that the ten signs God brought upon Egypt were punitive and redemptive. By punishing Egypt for their transgression, God gave them the opportunity for transformation and purification or death. He gave a similar choice to the Israelites in Deuteronomy 30:19 as He, through Moses, asked them to choose between life and death.

In John 2, we find that Yeshua's first public miracle was to turn the water into wine—a miraculous transformation. But unlike Moses and the bloody Nile, the result was a fine wine. In fact, the wedding guests commented that the best was saved for the final toast, not served during the wedding celebration. Yeshua, as greater than Moses, did not come to bring death. Instead, He came "that they might have life, and have it abundantly!" (John 10:10).

READ | Exodus 7:14-25; Deuteronomy 30:19; John 2:8-11; and John 10:10

REFLECT

1. In our study, we learned about biblical transformation. From what you learned, how would you define *transformation*?

> This miracle of water into wine illustrates that God wants to show up in counterintuitive ways. We need to expect the unexpected. He transformed the water into wine partly because water is ordinary, and wine is extraordinary. Turning the water into wine reflects the promise that God takes the ordinary and turns it into something extraordinary. He's a God who wants to bless us. He wants us to live in abundance.[3]

2. Our culture may not worship rivers, but what are some of the false gods that you've encountered in our contemporary society? Like the Egyptian worship of the Nile, how does this false worship harm people's lives and keep them from Jesus' transformation?

3. This first miracle of the water into wine is taking something ordinary and transforming it into something extraordinary. In Messiah, we become a new creation. The old will pass away and the new will come if we have faith. Can you recall events in your life that have caused transformation? What were the circumstances that caused the change?

The miracle of turning water into wine . . . was a miracle of blessing, abundance, and transformation. . . . However, transformation is not a one-and-done thing but rather a lifetime process of becoming. Personally, I am being transformed daily from something ordinary into something extraordinary. The old is passing away, and the new is coming into my life. I'm excited as I witness the things God is doing in me.[4]

4. How do you think that transformation through Yeshua has moved you from ordinary to having an extraordinary and abundant life?

5. Only Yeshua could turn ordinary water into extraordinary wine. This miracle is a clear picture of the transformation that only He can bring. God wants transformation in your life! No matter what you've done in the past, He forgives and transforms. Do you worry too much? Ask God to transform you from worry to faith and trust. Do you want to control things too much? Ask God to give you greater patience and gentleness. God can transform. How can He help you move from gruesome to gladness?

WHY 6 STONE POTS?

Every word and number in the Bible is significant. The Hebrew language is alphanumeric, which means numbers are represented by Hebrew letters. For example, *aleph* (א) is the first letter of the Hebrew alphabet and represents the number 1. *Beit* (ב) is the second letter and represents the number 2. The Hebrew letter *vav* (ו) is the 6th letter in the Hebrew alphabet and represents the number 6. In Jewish thinking, 6 is the number of connection.

So, what is significant about the number 6? In Jewish thought, 6 is the number of Creation. God worked for 6 days, then rested on the 7th day. 6 is the number of man. God created the first man and woman, Adam and Eve, on the 6th day of Creation. Man fell on the 6th day; Adam and Eve ate from the tree on the 6th day. We also need to remember that Yeshua died on the 6th day (Friday).

As previously noted, the number 6 is represented by the 6th letter of the Hebrew alphabet, *vav* (ו). This 6th letter is frequently used as a conjunction. For example, "God created the heavens and [*vav*] the earth." The Hebrew word *vav* means "connecting hook," and it's used as a connecting hook. For example, the curtains in the Tabernacle and Temple were attached by *vavim*—hooks—to the poles that supported them. It's also understood as the connecting hook between God and His people. It binds heaven and earth. God sent Yeshua to restore the connection between heaven and earth. Yeshua died on the 6th day. He restores, and His death transforms. He changed water into wine using 6 (*vav*) pots. He came to reconnect us to God.

Yeshua hung on the cross for 6 hours and was pierced in 6 places: His head was pierced with a crown of thorns (see John 19:2); His side was pierced (see John 19:32–35); His two hands were pierced (fulfilling Psalm 22:16–17); and his two feet were pierced (also fulfilling Psalm 22:16–17). Truly, using 6 pots was an intentional way for God to demonstrate the restored connection between Himself and humanity and His gift of redemption and transformation.

READ | John 2:6–7 and 2 Corinthians 5:17

REFLECT

1. The rabbis teach that it is "the wine that has been preserved in its grapes since the six days of creation."[5] There's good wine in the grapes that come from the garden of Eden and the 6 days of creation. The 6 stone pots point to the wine that has been preserved since those six days of Creation. How can this new wine lead you to new life and transformation? How does restoring the connection of the original fruitfulness and all that was lost at the Fall affect how we live today?

> There's yet another connection with the number 6 we should consider. This connection is not a restoration but a look forward. . . . Yeshua was giving the guests at the wedding at Cana a taste of the marriage supper of the Lamb, when the good wine would be served. It was a sneak preview of the abundant life to come.[6]

2. The wine was new but tasted old (which is good for quality wine). How can God take something old and supernaturally mature it? What are some ways you can become more supernaturally mature?

3. Combining something new with something old is also a sign of the coming Kingdom, when two different people groups, Jews and Gentiles, will unite. What would your community look like if the different people groups were able to unite?

If you rummage through your storage room or closet, you'll likely find that you have new and old items you treasure. What we often miss is the blessing when we bring both together. Maybe an old Bible with a new commentary. Or, more importantly, the truths of the Old Testament brought together with the truth of the New Testament.[7]

4. An everyday use for the stone pots was water storage, but God had a hidden treasure in mind. Sometimes, we forget the hidden treasures found in the Old Testament. What is the value of studying the Old Testament? What are you learning about how the truths of the Old Testament can be brought together with the truths of the New Testament?

5. Using water pots to create wine is certainly a counterintuitive method. It's not logical to think water can be turned into fine wine. But God often shows up in such counterintuitive ways. How has God shown up in your life and revealed a counterintuitive path to you? Reflect on 2 Corinthians 5:17 and God's extraordinary work to create a remarkable transformation you can personally experience.

PURIFICATION BEFORE TRANSFORMATION

In this week's teaching, you learned that purification is an important element of transformation. Something happens when God begins His work in us. We have old baggage. Old sins. Old thoughts. These need to be purged from us so that God can transform us into the new creation that He can use for His work and glory. Often, purging, or brokenness, proceeds to blessings. Purification, as a part of transformation, leads to freedom.

God redeemed the Children of Israel from slavery in Egypt at Passover, and the miracle of water into wine took place around Passover. Passover is about redemption, but redemption is not complete without transformation and purification. God brought Israel out of Egypt, but He had to take Egypt out of Israel. This purging is what leads to true freedom. It is for this reason that we see Yeshua in John 2:14–16 purging the Temple in Jerusalem.

Jesus, like His mother, Mary, showed some *chutzpah*, holy boldness, at the wedding. As we discussed in the group time, *chutzpah* can refer to bold actions, audacious behavior, courageous initiative, or plain old pushy nerve. Though it often has negative implications, we learn from Jewish tradition that *chutzpah* is a special gift from God and can be used in holy ways. God requires a certain kind of *chutzpah* from those who live for Him.

Yeshua went to the Temple to purify it at Passover. Passover is known as the Feast of Unleavened Bread, and all the leaven must be removed from the house. It was the responsibility of the children to help clean the house and prepare it for the Passover. The Temple was Yeshua's Father's house. He had to remove the leaven (representing sin). At that moment, Yeshua wasn't concerned about the leaven found in bread but about spiritual leaven. The physical removal of the "leaven" and cleaning the house for Passover symbolize that we must also be open to purification. Then we can be free to experience transformation.

READ | John 2:13–16; Philippians 3:12–14; and Isaiah 43:1–2

REFLECT

1. In this story, we find Yeshua offended and driving out the money changers as an act of purification. How would you describe God's purification?

2. By God's grace, He continues to purify and transform us. As you read Philippians 3:12–14, notice how Rabbi Paul attacked his transformation. How can his experience help you as God purifies you for transformation?

3. In Philippians 3:14, Paul uses the phrase "press on." He uses the Greek word *diōkō*, which metaphorically can mean "to seek after eagerly, earnestly endeavor to acquire."[8] What does this mean as it relates to how you should seek after God?

4. Another aspect of Paul's purification is forgetting what lies behind (see verse 13). How can we rid ourselves of continually thinking about mistakes from yesterday? How do guilt and condemnation steal our energy from reaching the goal of transformation?

5. There are several promises found in Isaiah 43:1–2. One is that anything God asks us to do, we can do it. He has our backs. How does this confidence in God help you on the journey of purification that leads to transformation?

CONNECT AND DISCUSS

Sometimes we need other people to help us absorb and learn. So take time this week to connect with a group member and discuss some of this session's insights and teaching. The following prompts can help guide your discussion.

1. How did this session help you see the importance of purification that leads to transformation?

2. What are some of the areas God has shown you that need to be purified? How can your study partner help?

3. How would you describe the significance of the six stone pots? How do you think understanding biblical numbers will change how you study the Bible?

CATCH UP AND READ AHEAD

Use this time to go back and complete any study and reflection questions from previous days this week that you weren't able to finish. Make a note below of any revelations you've had and reflect on any growth or personal insights you've gained.

Read chapters 3–4 in *Signs and Secrets of the Messiah* before the next group session. Make any notes below from your reading that stand out to you or encourage you.

WEEK 2

BEFORE GROUP MEETING	Read chapters 3–4 in *Signs and Secrets of the Messiah* Read the Welcome section (page 23)
GROUP MEETING	Discuss the Connect questions Watch the video teaching for session 2 Discuss the questions that follow as a group Do the closing exercise and pray (pages 23–28)
STUDY 1	Complete the personal study (pages 30–32)
STUDY 2	Complete the personal study (pages 33–34)
STUDY 3	Complete the personal study (pages 35–37)
CONNECT AND DISCUSS	Connect with someone in your group (page 38)
CATCH UP AND READ AHEAD (before week 3 group meeting)	Read chapters 5–6 in *Signs and Secrets of the Messiah* Complete any unfinished personal studies

THE SIGNS AND SECRETS OF THE NEW BIRTH

Yeshua answered him, "Amen, amen I tell you, unless one is born from above, he cannot see the kingdom of God."

JOHN 3:3

In the first session of *Signs and Secrets of the Messiah*, we considered Yeshua's first miracle of turning the water into wine and His cleansing of the Temple. These miracles and mysteries point to transformation and purification. Yeshua brought about a greater redemption than Moses, symbolized by turning the water into wine at the wedding in Cana. Yeshua takes something ordinary and makes it extraordinary—a new creation. That new creation transformation is available to us now, which is great news for all of us on our journey as Christians.

The cleansing of the Temple concerns itself with the miracle of purification and freedom. Yeshua was about His Father's business to clean up His Father's house. He did this during the Passover season as a reminder that Passover symbolizes Yeshua wanting to cleanse us and bring freedom and fullness to us as He washes away our past.

In this next session we will study John 3, where Yeshua encountered a Pharisee one-on-one. As you will discover, Nicodemus was one of the leading Pharisees of his day. He was in high standing and probably a wealthy man. The Pharisees derived their name from the Hebrew word *perushim*, or "separate," and they separated themselves from ritually impure food and from eating with the "common" people—people who didn't hold to rabbinic law and tithing.

It's this *perushim* that Yeshua encountered in John 3, where we learn about the new birth and why such a concept should not have been foreign to Nicodemus.

CONNECT | 15 MINUTES

Get the session started by choosing one of these questions to discuss as a group:

- What was something that spoke to your heart from last week's personal study that you would like to share with the group?

  — *or* —

- What immediately comes to mind when you think about the concept of being born again?

WATCH | 20 MINUTES

Now watch the video for this session. Below is an outline of the key points covered during the teaching. Record any concepts that stand out to you.

OUTLINE

I. A Pharisee named Nicodemus came to meet Yeshua at night (see John 3:1–13).
   A. Yeshua's beliefs and values were more closely aligned with the Pharisees than other religious sects (like the priests or Sadducees).
   B. The Pharisees prayed and worshiped three times a day.
   C. The Pharisees believed in the supernatural, the existence of angels, and the resurrection of the dead.
II. In Jewish sources, there was a man named Nicodemus ben Gurion.
   A. He is described as a wealthy Jew who lived in Jerusalem in the first century.
   B. He was a member of the Sanhedrin; a religious ruling body of ancient Israel.
III. The idea of being born again wasn't foreign to the rabbis.
   A. A Gentile who converts to Judaism is considered to be like a newborn child.
      1. In a sense, they are born anew into the Jewish faith.
      2. Some Jews thought that an actual supernatural birth happened when a Gentile converted to Judaism and believed in the God of Israel.
   B. There is spiritual significance in Nicodemus visiting Yeshua at night.
   C. Nicodemus was on a journey from dark to the light.
IV. Yeshua compared Himself to the serpent on the pole (see John 3:14–21).
   A. God commanded Moses to make a bronze serpent and lift it on a pole (see Numbers 21:4–9).
   B. When the people saw the serpent and looked up in faith, they would be healed.
   C. Yeshua would bear, or carry, our sin and guilt. It ties back to the Jewish system of atonement.
V. Yeshua spoke to Nicodemus on two levels.
   A. There are two aspects of the Torah in Jewish thought.
      1. The revealed Torah (*nigleh*).
      2. The hidden or concealed Torah (*nistar*).
   B. Yeshua was saying that if Nicodemus could not understand the "revealed" things of Scripture, how would he understand the "concealed" things—the deeper meanings?
   C. God conceals some things so we seek them out. He rewards those who diligently seek Him.

NOTES

DISCUSS | 35 MINUTES

Take time to discuss what you just watched by answering the following questions.

1. What were the circumstances of Nicodemus's visiting Yeshua? What do you think was Nicodemus's purpose?

2. Read aloud a parallel account in Luke 18:18-23. What do you think was the religious leader's motive for this question? What do you think Yeshua saw in his heart?

3. How would you put Yeshua's response to Nicodemus into your own words? How would you help Nicodemus understand the idea of being born again?

4. When Adam and Eve pulled down that fruit from the tree and disobeyed God's command, they dragged all of humanity and all of Creation down with them. How does Yeshua being "lifted up" overcome what happened in the garden of Eden? How does this idea of pulling down and lifting up apply to us today?

5. Why do you think God conceals some things from us? What is our reward when we diligently seek Him?

RESPOND | 10 MINUTES

In this session, you spent some time learning about the biblical principle of being born again. The teaching pointed out that the concept should not have been new to Nicodemus because the Jews thought that when a Gentile converted to Judaism they were "born again." Take a few moments to read the scriptures below and answer the questions that follow.

> Then I will sprinkle clean water on you and you will be clean from all your uncleanness and from all your idols. Moreover I will give you a new heart. I will put a new spirit within you. I will remove the stony heart from your flesh and give you a heart of flesh. I will put My RUACH [Spirit] within you. Then I will cause you to walk in My laws, so you will keep My rulings and do them.
>
> Ezekiel 36:25-27

> Jesus replied, "Very truly I tell you, no one can see the kingdom of God unless they are born again." "How can someone be born when they are old?" Nicodemus asked. "Surely they cannot enter a second time into their mother's womb to be born!" Jesus answered, "Very truly I tell you, no one can enter the kingdom of God unless they are born of water and the Spirit. Flesh gives birth to flesh, but the Spirit gives birth to spirit. You should not be surprised at my saying, 'You must be born again.'"
>
> John 3:3-7 NIV

What are some of the key words in these verses that help describe being born again? Take time to highlight them and discuss their meaning.

Have you been born again? If so, how has being born again affected your life?

PRAY | 10 MINUTES

End your time by praying together. Ask God to create moments when you can share your "born again" story with others outside your group and help them see how being born again through the Spirit has changed your life. Also, ask if any of the members have prayer requests to share. Write those requests along with the names of people whom you're praying for below so you and group members can continue to pray about them in the week ahead.

Name   **Request**

PERSONAL STUDY

In this week's group time, you explored the story of a Pharisee's encounter with Yeshua. Nicodemus had some questions regarding Yeshua's teaching about being born again. He came by night (for several reasons) and confronted Yeshua, who pointed to his lack of understanding of what the Hebrew Bible said about being born again and the Jewish custom for Gentile conversion into Judaism. Yeshua used a story from the Old Testament book of Numbers to help clarify and perhaps help Nicodemus remember his study of Scripture. As you work through each day's study, write down your responses to the questions, as you will be given a few minutes to share your insights at the start of the next session (if you are doing this study with others). If you are reading *Signs and Secrets of the Messiah*, first review chapters 3 and 4 in the book.

WHY AT NIGHT?

In this week's teaching, Nicodemus was described as a wealthy Pharisee, a member of the Sanhedrin, and a man who had witnessed signs and miracles. His name in Greek means victory and breakthrough. Why, then, would this man come to Yeshua at *night*? Why wouldn't he use his power and influence to meet Yeshua at any time and place?

The reason is because Nicodemus had a lot to lose. The religious rulers of that day were not drawn to Yeshua. Their attitude was quite the opposite. As Charles Swindoll wrote, "Jesus was not the kind of Messiah those scholars and priests were looking for. They had no interest in personal righteousness; they were concerned only with political power. They had no time for national repentance; they were looking only for military might. They weren't longing for peace, justice, and mercy; they cared only about their own economic prosperity. If the Messiah came for anything other than their own personal gain, they weren't interested."[9]

So Nicodemus risked a lot to come to Yeshua, and he did so in the dark. He didn't realize that he would be traveling from the darkness to the light of the Messiah. There is a spiritual symbolism in this idea of night. In one sense, Nicodemus was in the dark because he didn't know who Yeshua was. But in Jewish thought, night represents exile, and light represents redemption. During their Egyptian exile, the Israelites were symbolically living in the dark. Through Moses, God led them out of this darkness and confinement into the light of freedom.

Yeshua took on spiritual darkness to redeem us from exile and darkness during His three hours of darkness on the cross. He withstood the darkness of the cross so that we could go from darkness into light. Nicodemus was on that journey—from the dark to the light.

READD | Deuteronomy 7:7-8; Matthew 21:14-17; and John 3:1-3

REFLECT

1. Why do you think that Nicodemus, a highly trained religious leader, was in the dark? Why do you think many religiously trained people choose to be in spiritual darkness?

In Genesis 1, we see "there was evening and there was morning—one day" (verse 5). Amid the darkness, God said, "Let there be light!" (verse 3). Just as Creation happened out of darkness, so people become new creations out of the darkness. The new creation has experienced salvation and is moving from the kingdom of darkness to the kingdom of light. Nicodemus was on a journey from darkness to light. He was moving from the place of formlessness and void and chaos. And God was about to say, "Let there be light!" The light bulb was going on within Nicodemus, and the night was about to give way to Yeshua's miracle of light and new birth.[10]

2. All of us experience times of darkness. Think about a time when you were in darkness and were looking for the light. What did it feel like to be in such darkness? What about spiritual darkness—how does that feel? How can you escape it and be in the light?

3. In Jewish thought, Egypt was a womb. The Hebrew word for Egypt (*Mitzrayim*) actually means "a place of confinement." How does living in the dark seem like confinement? How can spiritual darkness trap us into personal confinement?

4. Yeshua took the idea of darkness so that we could be free from spiritual exile. Describe how it feels in that freedom. Describe how you feel knowing what Yeshua did for you.

[At Mount Sinai], all the people witnessed the thunder, lightning flashes, sound of the trumpet, and mountain smoking. And when the people saw it, they trembled and stood far off. They all heard, saw, and stood. God brought healing to the people before they received the Torah. This directs us to understand that the wisdom of the Word of the Lord brings both physical and spiritual life and blessing.... *All* Israel mattered to God. God called *all* to be a holy priesthood in a royal nation.[11]

5. The Israelites emerging from Egypt meant being born from an enslaved people into a nation called to become a royal priesthood and a holy nation. How should these identities shape the nation of Israel? How do they shape your identity?

A SERPENT ON A POLE?

As you watched this week's teaching, it may have seemed strange to you that Yeshua would compare Himself to the serpent on a pole. Nicodemus himself might have shook his head when Yeshua made this analogy. So Yeshua recalled Numbers 21:4–7 to help him understand. He used the Bible to teach biblical concepts—how Nicodemus could receive eternal life.

This passage in Numbers shares a story from the Children of Israel's desert wanderings. They grumbled against God, so the Lord sent fiery serpents to bite them, and many of the people died. God then commanded Moses to make a bronze serpent and to lift it up on a pole. When the people saw the bronze serpent and looked up in faith, they were healed. Yeshua challenged Nicodemus to see the connection between what God did in the Old Testament and what He would do at Yeshua's crucifixion when He offered healing and salvation.

As Warren Wiersbe wrote, "The comparisons between the bronze serpent in Moses' day and the cross of Christ help us better understand the meaning of God's grace in salvation. All people have been infected by sin and will one day die and face judgment (Hebrews 9:27), but if they look by faith to Christ, He will save them and give them eternal life. Looking to the bronze serpent saved people from physical death, but looking to Christ saves us from eternal death."[12]

But there's more. We must dig deeper into the phrase "lifted up" (*nasa* in Hebrew). In the Hebrew version of the New Testament, the serpent in the wilderness was "lifted up" (*nasa*) and bore the sins of the grumbling people. Yeshua was also "lifted up" on the cross. He bore our sins and pains. Just like the people who looked at the serpent on the pole found healing, when we look to Yeshua Jesus on the cross, we find healing and wholeness.

READ | Numbers 21:4–9; Isaiah 53:4; and John 3:14–15

REFLECT

1. Yeshua was speaking to an important Pharisee. Why do you think it was significant for Him to talk about the Old Testament story of the serpent on the pole?

The Hebrew word [*nasa*] can mean "to lift up," but it can also mean "to bear," "to carry," or "to forgive." The meaning in John 3:14 is "to bear" or "to carry" sin and guilt. In the Jewish system of atonement, a scapegoat was offered in the Temple, on the Day of Atonement, to make atonement for the people; the goat carried the sins of the people: "The goat will carry [*nasa*] all their iniquities by itself into a solitary land and he is to leave the goat in the wilderness" (Leviticus 16:22).[13]

2. In Numbers 21:7, the Children of Israel asked Moses to pray for them. They knew the answer to their challenge was to be found in prayer. How does this request show their dependence on God? How has prayer increased your dependence on God?

3. The bronze serpent gives us an image of evil that is judged and dealt with. How does this image compare to what Yeshua did on the cross? How does the work of the cross carry us today?

4. Eternal life means much more than just never-ending life. What does the phrase "eternal life" mean to you? Why do you think people have trouble telling others about the eternal life that Yeshua offers?

5. Isaiah 53:4 relates the idea of Yeshua "carrying" (*nasa*) our pain. Jesus offers to carry your pains. How can that promise help you to live a more joy-filled life?

SEARCHING FOR DEEPER TRUTHS

Yeshua spoke to Nicodemus on two levels. One was the simple or plain level of teaching, and the other was a deeper level. Yeshua said to Nicodemus that if he couldn't understand the simple things, how would he know the deeper ones? This comment is based on Deuteronomy 29:28, when Moses spoke some of his last words to the Children of Israel. Yeshua asked Nicodemus to consider going deeper and not merely looking at the surface or the simple. After all, as we've discussed, Nicodemus was a Pharisee and was learned in the Torah.

God revealed many things to the Children of Israel—and the Law was one of them. This idea is relevant to us as we study and learn from the Bible. We should always ask ourselves, *What is God revealing to me today as I read and study my Bible?* But we can't merely settle for the simple or plain truths. It should be our goal to uncover the hidden things of Scripture. It's like peeling an onion, removing layer after layer of God's truth, promises, and application to our lives. God does not hide the truth so that we can't find it. God hides the truth because He wants us to go deeper into our relationship with Him, His Word, and our faith to find it. When we dig deeper, meditate, and live out the revealed and the hidden truths, we draw closer to God. We invite His intimate presence into our daily lives.

Digging deeper into the truth of Scripture also helps us to connect the Old and New Testaments. Digging deeper causes us to make these connections, and we add significantly to the definition of our faith. We enlarge it as we see how God has worked in people's lives since the beginning. We find how He has kept His promises and His prophecies. We learn from Old Testament people and better understand how and why the disciples reacted as they did—because they were Jewish and knew the Hebrew Scriptures. In essence, we rediscover our forgotten inheritance. Expanding our understanding of the hidden things in Scripture, including ancient Hebrew and contemporary wisdom informed by the Holy Spirit, enriches our perspective of Yeshua and His teaching.

READ | Deuteronomy 29:28; John 3:10–15; and Hebrews 11:6

REFLECT

1. Have you ever been on a scavenger hunt where you had to find a number of items on a list? What was it was like for you to find all that hidden "treasure"?

2. Think about your Bible study time. Do you tend to "dig for more" or just read for devotional purposes? Or both? What in this teaching prompts you to dig more?

> There are two aspects of the Torah: the revealed Torah (*nigleh*) and the hidden, or concealed, Torah (*nistar*). In other words, that which we can know, and the mystical. . . . In His explanation to Nicodemus about being born again, Yeshua essentially said, "Nicodemus, if you can't even comprehend the revealed things, how will you understand the deeper revelation of the concealed things?"[14]

3. Why can't we settle for the simple truths of the Bible? What could the concealed things reveal to us? How could they help us mature in our Christian lives?

> As children of the King, we can't just settle for the simple truths of Scripture. It is our glory to search out the concealed things, the deeper meanings, the deeper truths about Yeshua and the things He taught. That is the fusion of the old and the new coming together. When we search for deeper truths, we are not settling for half an inheritance. . . . Hebrews 11:6 says, "But without faith it is impossible to please Him, for he who comes to God must believe that He is, and that He is a rewarder of those who diligently seek Him" (NKJV). God rewards those who diligently seek Him.[15]

4. Some followers of Yeshua only focus on the New Testament writings. Why do you think it is so tempting to just settle for "half" an inheritance?

5. In Hebrews 11:6, we read that God rewards those who diligently seek Him. What are some of those rewards that you've experienced in your life? What is the most important reward for digging deeper into God's Word for the hidden truth?

CONNECT AND DISCUSS

Take some time today to connect with a group member and discuss some insights from this session. Use any of the prompts below to guide your discussion.

1. Describe Nicodemus. Why do you think he chose to come and talk to Jesus?

2. Coming out of the darkness into light is an exciting concept. What does this mean, and why is it important to help people see the light of Messiah Yeshua?

3. Nicodemus should have known the concept of being born again. So why do you think Yeshua's words stumped him on that point?

CATCH UP AND READ AHEAD

Use this time to go back and complete any study and reflection questions from previous days this week that you weren't able to finish. Make a note below of any revelations you've had and reflect on any growth or personal insights you've gained.

Read chapters 5–6 in *Signs and Secrets of the Messiah* before the next group session. Use the space below to make note of anything that stands out to you or encourages you from your reading.

WEEK 3

BEFORE GROUP MEETING	Read chapters 5–6 in *Signs and Secrets of the Messiah* Read the Welcome section (page 43)
GROUP MEETING	Discuss the Connect questions Watch the video teaching for session 3 Discuss the questions that follow as a group Do the closing exercise and pray (pages 43–48)
STUDY 1	Complete the personal study (pages 50–52)
STUDY 2	Complete the personal study (pages 53–55)
STUDY 3	Complete the personal study (pages 56–57)
CONNECT AND DISCUSS	Connect with someone in your group (page 58)
CATCH UP AND READ AHEAD (before week 4 group meeting)	Read chapters 7–8 in *Signs and Secrets of the Messiah* Complete any unfinished personal studies

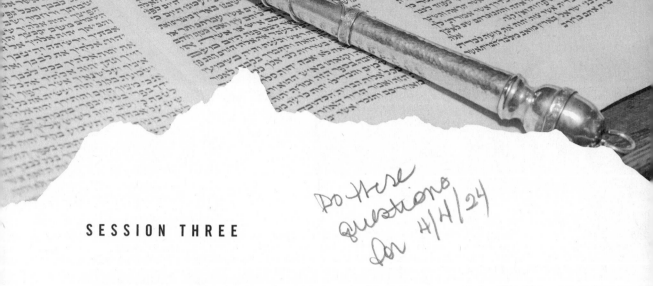

Do these questions for 4/4/24

THE SIGNS AND SECRETS OF HEALING

Seeing him lying there and knowing he had been that way a long time, Yeshua said to him, "Do you want to get well?"

JOHN 5:6

WELCOME | READ ON YOUR OWN

Shalom, and welcome to session three of the *Signs and Secrets of the Messiah*. We covered a lot of ground in the first two sessions. We walked through Yeshua's miracles in the Gospel of John of turning water into wine, the cleansing of the Temple, and, in our last session, the signs and secrets surrounding Nicodemus's visit to Yeshua and their discussion about the new birth.

Turning water into wine established Yeshua's identity as the greater than Moses. While Moses turned the Nile into blood, a symbol of death, Yeshua came to bring life, turning water into extraordinary wine. We also can't overlook Mary and her "holy boldness" as she saw the need, spoke to her Son, and directed the servants. We also studied the concept of moving from darkness into light as we explored the exchange between Yeshua and Nicodemus. The new birth offers the invitation to live in the light of Yeshua's redemption and love.

In this session, we will examine two miracles related to healing and wholeness. In John 5, Yeshua encountered a man who had been unable to walk for thirty-eight years. He asked the man what could seem like a rhetorical question: "Do you want to be well?" However, the question had a deeper meaning that we will explore, along with why Yeshua chose not only to heal on a Jewish holiday but also on a Sabbath—both of which contradicted Jewish law.

We will also explore the miracle of Yeshua healing a nobleman's son from a distance. This man showed incredible faith and trust in Yeshua, and the results were miraculous. Yeshua healed the man's son, speaking a word just as God spoke the world into existence. These miracles reveal that when we submit to Yeshua and allow Him to transform us, He fills us with emotional, spiritual, relational, and physical healing and wholeness.

CONNECT | 15 MINUTES

Get the session started by choosing one of these questions to discuss as a group:

- What is something that spoke to your heart in last week's personal study that you would like to share with the group?

  — *or* —

- When was the last time you hesitated to do something critical for your emotional or physical health? What were your reasons for waiting?

WATCH | 20 MINUTES

Now watch the video for this session. Below is an outline of the key points covered during the teaching. Record any key concepts that stand out to you.

OUTLINE

I. Yeshua healed a man beside a pool near the sheep gate (see John 5:1–13).
   A. The blind, lame, and disabled near this gate were not considered as valuable as sheep.
   B. They were like sheep without a shepherd.
   C. Yeshua cared about these broken sheep who were societal outcasts.

II. Yeshua asked one man who was there, "Do you want get well?" (verse 6).
   A. The man offered Yeshua an excuse.
   B. The man felt stuck, hopeless, and without a future.
   C. Hope is the belief that your future is going to be better than your past.

III. The Jewish leaders could not understand why Yeshua would heal the man on Pentecost (the *Shabbat*) and on the Sabbath (see John 5:16–18).
   A. Pentecost is a celebration of hope.
   B. Pentecost is when the Children of Israel received the Ten Commandments (see Exodus 20) and the disciples received the Holy Spirit (see Acts 2).
   C. The numbers 5 and 3 are important to our understanding of this miracle.

IV. Yeshua healed a nobleman's son from a distance (see John 4:43–54).
   A. Yeshua performed both His first and second miracles in Cana.
   B. When Scripture mentions Cana, it's always in connection to the Galilee because it is meant to be a fulfillment of prophecy.
   C. The meaning of Cana connects back to Creation.

V. The Lord wants you to experience healing and wholeness in Him.
   A. Sin creates a vacuum within people.
   B. If that void is not filled with God, we reach for false attractions that enslave and destroy us.
   C. In both miracles, sickness was transformed into health and death was transformed into life.

NOTES

DISCUSS | 35 MINUTES

Now discuss what you just watched by answering the following questions.

1. The man by the pool felt utterly hopeless. Have you ever felt as if nothing would ever change for you? How did God created hopefulness for you in that situation?

2. According to Jewish tradition, before the Lord gave His people the Torah at Mount Sinai, He healed them and gave them wholeness. Why do you think it was important for God to heal the Children of Israel *before* they received the Ten Commandments?

3. In John 4, we read that Yeshua healed the nobleman's son from a distance. Why do you think Yeshua didn't go to Capernaum to heal the son directly? What can we learn from this miracle of Yeshua's "distance healing"?

4. The Hebrew word for sickness, at its root, means "to hollow out" or "to bore out." Sickness then creates a vacuum. Since a vacuum can't remain void or empty, how do people tend to fill this vacuum?

5. Have you experienced situations like the lame man or the nobleman? How do Yeshua's miracles give you hope and freedom? How has God filled you with healing and wholeness from spiritual, emotional, relational, and physical "holes"?

RESPOND | 10 MINUTES

Our God wants us to experience wholeness in the name of Yeshua. He deeply desires us to "get up and walk" in His will and ways. Of course, getting up and walking doesn't mean there won't be challenges along the way. But we can know that every time we are pushed down or discouraged, our God will be there, for He is the God of hope. Reflect on these truths as you read the scripture below, and then answer the questions that follow.

> *Chazak!* Be courageous! Do not be afraid or tremble before them. For ADONAI your God—He is the One who goes with you. He will not fail you or abandon you." Then Moses summoned Joshua and said to him in the sight of all Israel, "Be strong! Be courageous! For you are to go with this people into the land ADONAI has sworn to their fathers to give them, and you are to enable them to inherit it. ADONAI —He is the One who goes before you. He will be with you. He will not fail you or abandon you."
>
> Deuteronomy 31:6-8

What does Moses reiterate about God's presence? What does he say they are to remember as they go into the land that God promised to their forefathers?

Did God stir anything in you this week as you learned about the healing and wholeness that only Yeshua provides? If so, what did He bring to your mind?

PRAY | 10 MINUTES

End your time by praying together as a group. As you pray, ask God to show you ways in which you might feel His healing touch and hopefulness. Ask the Lord to help you move from healing to wholeness. Ask if anyone has prayer requests and write those in the space below so that you and your group members can continue to pray about them in the week ahead.

Name   **Request**

_____   _____

_____   _____

_____   _____

_____   _____

_____   _____

_____   _____

_____   _____

_____   _____

_____   _____

_____   _____

PERSONAL STUDY

As you learned in this week's teaching, Yeshua wants to bring healing and wholeness into your life. He wants you to know that you can't merely lie out by the pool. He wants you to get up and walk! In the personal studies this week, you will go a bit deeper into some of the teachings from the group time. As you work through each day's study, write down your responses to the questions, as you will be given a few minutes to share your insights at the start of the next session (if you are doing this study with others). If you are reading *Signs and Secrets of the Messiah* while doing this study, first review chapters 5 and 6 in the book.

A DOUBLE MISTAKE?

In this week's group time, you discussed the controversy of Yeshua healing on a holiday (probably *Shavuot*/Pentecost) and on the Sabbath. In Judaism, there are three pilgrimage holidays: (1) Passover, or *Pesach*; (2) *Shavuot*, or Pentecost; and (3) *Sukkot*, the Feast of Tabernacles. While John doesn't specifically tell us which holiday this is, there are several reasons why it's likely *Shavuot*. The Gospels frequently mention Passover, so John probably would have mentioned that as he did in other places. *Sukkot* is a festival, and that term isn't used in John 5. Pentecost begins seven full weeks, or exactly fifty days after the Feast of Firstfruits (or Weeks, the second evening of Passover), so it is likely the holiday John mentions.

Pentecost is one of the spring holidays. It combines two religious observances—the early summer grain harvest and the giving of the Torah to Moses on Mount Sinai. The focus of Pentecost is on revelation and hope. During Jesus' time on earth, He gave the gift of the Holy Spirit to the disciples in Jerusalem on Pentecost. There is something significant about the fact that God chose the same day, both in the Old and New Testaments, to give the gift of Word and Spirit. Word and Spirit combine to bring us greater revelation and hope. There's always hope.

The Sabbath (*Shabbat* in Hebrew) is the first holiday that God put on the Jewish people's calendar. The focus of this day (celebrated from sundown on Friday to sunset on Saturday) is to rest, remember, and restore. In fact, the Hebrew word *Shabbat* means "to rest" or "put an end to." Remember, God rested on the seventh day. Observing *Shabbat* is about mastering time to rest and deepen our relationship with God and others.

Just as God healed on the first *Shavuot* (which also happened to be a Sabbath in many Jewish scholars' opinions) before giving the people the Ten Commandments, so Yeshua followed in His footsteps. In John 5, He openly declared His relationship with His Father. He made it clear that He was doing His Father's work and not His own—and that He would do that work on the Sabbath or any day of the week. He responded to a person's need.

READ | Leviticus 23:1–3 and John 5:19–25

REFLECT

1. Helping someone in need is generally seen as a good thing. So why were the Jewish leaders upset with Yeshua healing on a holiday? What do you think was the hidden reason?

> There was a certain man at the pool who could not walk. Yeshua asked him, "Do you want to get well?" That seems like a crazy question. Of course! Who wouldn't want to get well? This guy had been unable to walk for thirty-eight years. Life expectancy in the first century was only about forty. He'd lived his entire life without the ability to walk and had lost hope. Hal Lindsey has been quoted as saying, "Man can live about forty days without food, about three days without water, about eight minutes without air, but only for one second without hope."[16] . . . This man was hopeless.[17]

2. *Shavuot*/Pentecost is a holiday of revelation and hope. God wants to reveal things to you to help you grow and mature in Him. He also wants to move you from hopelessness to healing and wholeness. How would you define what *hope* means?

> In John 5, when Yeshua healed the man, the religious leaders were upset because it was on *Shabbat* (the Sabbath). . . . Why is healing on the Sabbath so significant? It wasn't just to give the Judean leaders an excuse to persecute Him. All this connects to the giving of the Torah on Mount Sinai. There are two opinions in Jewish tradition. Some say God gave the Torah on the sixth day of the week, which is Friday. Others say God gave the Torah on the sixth of *Sivan* (May–June), which happened to be a Friday, the sixth day of the week. The day God gave the Torah was a *Shabbat* or was just going into the *Shabbat* (a Saturday). Yeshua healed on the *Shabbat* just like God healed on *Shabbat* at Sinai according to Jewish tradition. Yeshua was saying in John 5, "Look, I'm the Son. I can only do what I see My Father doing." The Father commanded healing on the first *Shavuot*, the first Pentecost. So Yeshua also healed on Pentecost.[18]

3. *Shabbat*/Sabbath is a time of rest and reflection. Why do you think it is important that we set aside time to rest and reflect as our Father Creator did? How could you make more time in your weeks and days for rest and reflection?

4. "*Yeshua* answered them, 'Amen, amen I tell you, the Son cannot do anything by Himself. He can do only what He sees the Father doing. Whatever the Father does, the Son does likewise'" (John 5:19). How was Yeshua's healing of the man beside the pool—which led to the man's wholeness—doing what His Father was doing?

5. We can often become confined by our own "laws and traditions." How can that trap keep you from helping others in need? What are some ways that you could break free of this kind of confinement to help others who need the hope and revelation of Yeshua?

THE NUMBERS 5, 3, AND 38

During this week's group time, you examined three numbers in Scripture concerning healing and wholeness. Remember that every word in Scripture is God-breathed (see 2 Timothy 3:16), even the numbers, so there's significance in every number in the Bible. As previously explained, Hebrew and Greek are both alphanumeric. This means that letters represent numbers—the first letter of the Hebrew alphabet is *aleph*, and it is also the number 1, and so on.

The 5th Hebrew letter, *hei* (ה), is also the number 5. The number 5 gives us a few clues about the holiday in which Yeshua performed the healing from this session. John mentions 5 porches (see John 5:2). On the first *Shavuot*/Pentecost, God came down from Mount Sinai and spoke the Ten Commandments. These commandments were written by God's finger on two tablets, with 5 commands each. During *Shavuot*, Jewish people celebrate the 5 books of Moses.

5 is the number of grace and mercy. God gave His covenant as an act of grace. As you saw in this week's teaching, the number 5 also ties to the words for Bethesda, *Beit Chesed* in Hebrew, or *Bethzatha* in Aramaic. These names mean "house of loving-kindness or grace." It's a place for healing and wholeness. Interestingly, God changed Abram's name to Abraham and Sarai to Sarah (see Genesis 17:5, 15). He made this change by inserting in the middle a *hei*, or the 5th letter, changing Abram to Abra**h**am, Sarai to Sara**h**. This name change happened on the Lord's 5th visit to Abraham and showed that they walked in God's grace and mercy.

The number 3 is also important in this week's teaching. There were 3 types of people at the pool: blind, lame, and disabled. Yeshua commanded the man to do 3 things: "Get up! Pick up your mat and walk!" (John 5:8). God gave the Torah on the 3rd day of the 3rd month through the thirdborn, Moses. The Hebrew Bible is divided into 3 parts: the Torah (Law), the Writings, and the Prophets. The number 3 also denotes divine perfection—the Trinity.

The man at the pool had been an invalid for 38 years, which is also an important number. 38 is the numerical value of "His heart," or the Hebrew word *libo* (לבּוֹ, or the Hebrew letters *lamed* [30] + *beit* [2] + *vav* [6] = 38). By asking the man if he wanted to be well,

Yeshua was testing his heart. The Children of Israel wandered for 38 years. They kept testing God along the way. Yeshua didn't want this man's heart to be a grumbling heart with an enslaved mentality. The man didn't need to be a victim but was to be victorious through healing and wholeness.

READ | Genesis 17:4-7; Deuteronomy 2:14; and John 5:1-9

REFLECT

1. "Both words and numbers are significant as we study the mysteries and secrets in the Bible."[19] What have you learned so far in this study about the significance of numbers in the Bible? How can an understanding of numbers change how you study Scripture?

2. 5 in Hebrew is considered the number of grace and mercy. In your own words, how would you define *grace* and *mercy*? How was Yeshua's healing of the man an act of grace and mercy?

Let's look at the number 38. People often recount that the Israelites wandered in the desert for 40 years (see Deuteronomy 2:14). Well, that's true and not true. Yes, they were in the desert for 40 years, but 38 years were because of their unbelief. . . . John recorded this miracle partly to demonstrate that this victim mentality doesn't have to happen to us. There is hope if we believe and have faith in the greater than Moses, the Messiah, Yeshua. Yeshua healed this man, and He can heal us.[20]

3. The significance of the number 38—the number of years the man was an invalid beside the pool—relates to the Israelites' wandering in the wilderness. How many years did they wander because of *unbelief*? Why did they need to wander that long when the trip to the Promised Land could have been eleven days?

God's creative power and healing flowed through this man at the pool of Bethesda. He didn't have to die in isolation. Yeshua essentially said, "Do you want to be like the generation that came out of Egypt, who died after 38 years? Do you want to die in this state? Or do you want to get up and walk and follow Me and obey?" Israel disobeyed, so they died in the wilderness. This man had to make a choice. So do we.[21]

4. What evidence do you see in the story told in John 5:1–9 that the man beside the pool had little hope that he would ever get well? How did Yeshua break through to him?

5. By asking the man if he wanted to be well, Yeshua was testing him to see what was in his heart. When was a time in your life that God "tested" your heart?

FILLING THE VOID

In Genesis 1:1–2, we read, "In the beginning, God created the heavens and the earth. The earth was without form and void, and darkness was over the face of the deep" (ESV). Some English translations replace the word *void* with *chaos*. Sin, at its root, leads to sickness because it creates a vacuum, or void, within people and all Creation. Adam and Eve were whole in the beginning, but they sinned, creating an empty space (or disconnect) between us and God. This disconnect led to a void, chaos, and lack of order. We were exiled and in need of redemption.

A quick understanding of Hebrew can help us understand how redemption fills that void and chaos. The first letter of the Hebrew alphabet is *aleph*. Consequently, its numerical value is 1. *Aleph* represents God's name. Most of the Hebrew names of God begin with the letter *aleph*—*Elohim* and *Adonai* are examples. Its numerical value alludes to the oneness of God.

There is a difference between exile and redemption. The Hebrew word for redemption is *gā'al*. The Hebrew word for exile is *gâlâh*. There's only one letter difference in Hebrew between the words—the letter *aleph*. When you remove God and take Him out of the equation, *exile* remains. Exile is about disconnection and distance. When we take God out of our lives—when we remove Him from society and culture—it should be no surprise that we see disconnection and chaos as a result. Disconnection leads to death and a broken, chaotic world. The world becomes *tōhû*, "formless and void," when we remove the *aleph* (God).

We reverse exile and turn to our needed redemption by putting the *aleph* back into the equation. We invite God to return to our lives and make Him our number 1 (*aleph*) priority. When we do, that's when redemption fills the earth. As Zechariah 14:9 says, "Adonai [the Lord] will then be King over all the earth. In that day Adonai will be *Echad* [One] and His Name *Echad*." The fullness of redemption will be when God is one, and we are one in Him, symbolized by the letter *aleph*. Now, more than ever, we need to be like the *aleph* and be one in Messiah. We need to let Him fill the void and remove the chaos that is in our lives.

READ | Genesis 1:1–4; John 4:50; Ephesians 1:7; and Colossians 1:14

REFLECT

1. What does it mean to be redeemed and freed from exile? Is there anything currently holding you in exile from God? (If so, declare now that Yeshua Messiah has redeemed you and freed you from anything that holds you in captivity.)

2. The Hebrew letter *aleph* represents the name of God and Yeshua. Just like the difference between the words *exile* and *redemption* in Hebrew, what differences could be made in other circumstances in our lives if we "inserted" the *aleph* into them?

3. When we put Yeshua, the *aleph*, into our situations and make Him the chief of our lives, we find genuine peace that fill the voids in our lives. How have you witnessed this to be true in your life? In what areas do you still need to receive Yeshua's peace?

4. Each of us has a void in our lives. What happens when we do not fill that void with God? What are some of the attractions that create a void or keep a void from being filled?

5. How did God adding light to Creation overcome the darkness? How can we help others see the light that will help them overcome the darkness in their lives?

CONNECT AND DISCUSS

Take some time today to connect with a group member and discuss some insights from this session. Use any of the prompts below to guide your discussion.

1. What new insights did you gain about healing and wholeness this week?

2. In which areas of your life do you need to move from chaos to wholeness?

3. What practical changes will you make beginning this week to help you move from exile to redemption?

CATCH UP AND READ AHEAD

Use this time to go back and complete any study and reflection questions from previous days this week that you weren't able to finish. Make a note below of any revelations you've had and reflect on any growth or personal insights you've gained.

Read chapters 7–8 in *Signs and Secrets of the Messiah* before the next group session. Use the space below to make note of anything that stands out to you or encourages you from your reading.

WEEK 4

BEFORE GROUP MEETING	Read chapters 7–8 in *Signs and Secrets of the Messiah* Read the Welcome section (page 63)
GROUP MEETING	Discuss the Connect questions Watch the video teaching for session 4 Discuss the questions that follow as a group Do the closing exercise and pray (pages 63–68)
STUDY 1	Complete the personal study (pages 70–71)
STUDY 2	Complete the personal study (pages 72–74)
STUDY 3	Complete the personal study (pages 75–77)
CONNECT AND DISCUSS	Connect with someone in your group (page 78)
CATCH UP AND READ AHEAD (before week 5 group meeting)	Read chapters 9–10 in *Signs and Secrets of the Messiah* Complete any unfinished personal studies

THE SIGNS AND SECRETS OF MULTIPLICATION

Lifting up His eyes and seeing a large crowd coming to Him, Yeshua said to Philip, "Where will we buy bread so these may eat?" Now Yeshua was saying this to test him, for He knew what He was about to do.

JOHN 6:5–6

In the previous session, we looked at the miracle of Yeshua healing a man who had lain by the pool of Bethesda for thirty-eight years. Yeshua asked him, "Do you want to get well?" (John 5:6) and then instructed him, "Get up! Pick up your mat and walk!" (verse 8). Those were wise words back then, and they are wise words for us to ponder today.

We also looked at the Hebrew word for sickness, *choleh*, and discussed how at its root, it means "to make a hole" or "to hollow or bore out." In the Hebrew understanding, sickness occurs when something is missing that should be there—when a *void* is present. Humanity was whole in the beginning, but when Adam and Eve sinned, it created a void (a disconnect) between us and God. A void will not stay open for long—something will fill it. We can choose between allowing God to fill the voids in our lives or filling them with harmful attractions.

In this session, we will examine the signs and secrets of multiplication. The story for this miracle comes from John 6, where Yeshua feeds a crowd of people with only five loaves of bread and two fish. In this teaching, we will explore Yeshua's testing of the disciples and see how it compares to God's testing of the Children of Israel in the wilderness.

We will also look a story told in John 9 that explores the signs and secrets of sight. In this account, we read that as "*Yeshua* was passing by, He saw a man who had been blind since birth" (verse 1). Just as Yeshua took the time to care for the needs of the crowd that had come to see Him, so He took the time to meet this man's needs and heal him. Yeshua didn't merely walk past people. He stopped to help the hurting and the lost. We will also discover that Yeshua used an unusual method to heal this man born blind. In the same way, Yeshua will often instruct us to take a unique path to walk us through our blindness and other challenges.

CONNECT | 15 MINUTES

Get the session started by choosing one of these questions to discuss as a group:

- What is something that spoke to your heart from last week's personal study that you would like to share with the group?

— *or* —

- When have you read a certain passage of Scripture and your eyes were opened anew to what God was teaching you?

WATCH | 20 MINUTES

Now watch the video for this session. Below is an outline of the key points covered during the teaching. Record any thoughts or concepts that stand out to you.

OUTLINE

I. Yeshua fed a crowd of 5,000 with five loaves and two fish (see John 6:1–15).
   A. The first thing we see is that Yeshua tested His disciples.
   B. It is important to understand this miracle happened around Passover.
   C. Yeshua tested the disciples much like God tested the Children of Israel in the wilderness.

II. The five loaves and two fish reveal the mystery of the number 7.
   A. On five days of the week, God gave the Children of Israel manna in the desert.
   B. They collected a double portion on the sixth day to last for two days.
   C. The number 7 symbolizes trusting God to possess your promise in the face of the improbable.

III. The Hebrew word for bread is *lechem*, and it connects to redemption.
   A. Passover celebrates Israel's redemption from Egypt.
   B. There is messianic significance to the number 90.
      1. The Hebrew word for *king* has a numerical value of 90.
      2. The numerical value of *manna* in Hebrew has a value of 90.
      3. 90 is also the numerical value in Hebrew of the words lambs, redemption, and *tzadik*.
   C. Yeshua's teachings become the foundation of the new covenant as the greater than Moses.

IV. We can't solve our problems by purely natural means.
   A. Too often we try to solve significant problems with our own meager resources apart from God.
   B. The more we rely on God and not on our wisdom, the more God will multiply what He has given to us.
   C. God blesses what we have in our hand, even if it's five loaves and two fish.

V. Yeshua healed a man who had been born blind (see John 9:1–34).
   A. This man born blind represents the religious leaders who were spiritually blind.
   B. The hurts we face frequently blind our ability to see correctly.
   C. Unless God opens our eyes by grace, we remain blind and in unbelief.

NOTES

DISCUSS | 35 MINUTES

Now discuss what you just watched by answering the following questions.

1. Read John 6:5–7. When Yeshua tests us, He always has our growth and our maturity as His followers in mind. According to these verses, what was Yeshua's motive was for this testing? How does this shed light on how God "tests" us?

2. When Yeshua asked Philip where they would buy bread, the disciple exclaimed, "Two hundred denarii isn't enough to buy bread for each to get a little bit!" (verse 7). Philip saw only the impossibility of the request. In your life, how has God presented you with situations that you first thought impossible to resolve?

3. Philip could not see an answer. Andrew, for his part, said to Yeshua, "There's a boy here who has five barley loaves and two fish—*but what's that for so many*?" (verse 9, emphasis added). How did Yeshua use this less-than-faith-filled response from Andrew to do something miraculous that day? What does this reveal about the way God uses our faith—no matter how great or small it may be?

4. Read Exodus 16:22. This miracle happened around Passover, a time in which the Jewish people remember when Moses led the Children of Israel out of Egypt. According to this verse, the Lord gave the Children of Israel a double portion of manna on the sixth day. They had to trust and rest in Him that the double portion would not rot. How do you likewise find ways to trust and rest in the Lord?

5. Unless God opens our eyes, we remain spiritually blinded by unbelief. What are some ways God has opened your eyes to Him and His will?

RESPOND | 10 MINUTES

It can be difficult to trust in God for His provision. Whether it is a financial challenge, a personal struggle, or wisdom that we need for His direction, asking God first is not typically something that we do. But God is waiting for us to ask! He is working all things together for our good (see Romans 8:28). Not only does He want us to trust Him for provision and multiplication, but He also wants us not to be blinded. He wants us to open our eyes and see Him.

> Now a natural man does not accept the things of the *Ruach Elohim* [Holy Spirit], for they are foolishness to him; and he cannot understand them, because they are spiritually discerned. But the one who is spiritual discerns all things, and he himself is discerned by no one. For "who has known the mind of ADONAI, that he will instruct Him?" But we have the mind of Messiah.
>
> 1 Corinthians 2:14–16

What does Paul say in this passage about spiritual blindness? How would you describe the difference between "a natural man" and a person who walks with the Holy Spirit?

Did God stir anything in you this week as you learned about the abundance and spiritual sight that Yeshua provides? If so, what did He bring to your mind?

PRAY | 10 MINUTES

End your time by praying together. Ask God to give you His "eyes" to see what He is doing in your life, to help you be open to the work that He wants to do within you, and to reveal that you can trust Him in the process. Also ask if anyone has prayer requests and write those in the space below so you and your group can continue to pray about them in the week ahead.

Name   **Request**

PERSONAL STUDY

As you heard and saw in this week's group time, God often tests us to train us so that He can conform us to His image, His will, and His ways. In the personal studies for this week, we will go a bit deeper into this idea of trusting God for His provision. We will uncover what the Bible says about trust, faith, and having eyes that see what God wants us to see—not merely what we see or the blindness that often affects our walk with Him. As you work through each day's study, write down your responses to the questions, as you will be given a few minutes to share your insights at the start of the next session (if you are doing this study with others). If you are reading *Signs and Secrets of the Messiah*, first review chapters 7 and 8 in the book.

TESTING AND TRAINING

It's interesting to read in John 6 that Yeshua *tested* His disciples. To give some context, a large crowd was following Yeshua. Passover was near, and "Yeshua went up the mountainside and sat down with His disciples" (verse 3). Yeshua looked at the large crowd and asked Philip, "Where will we buy bread so these may eat?" (verse 5). This was a critical moment for Philip. The question forced him to search his heart to see where he was placing his trust. Yeshua wanted to see if Philip would have the faith to believe when the situation seemed impossible.

There are many stories in the Bible in which God likewise asked someone to demonstrate faith, trust, and obedience in Him. Before looking at another example, let's be clear on definitions. *Faith* involves belief, while *trust* requires action. You can have faith in something, but if you don't act on it, there's no trust attached to that faith. With God, faith should lead to trust in Him, and the action should be obedience to His voice.

Abraham is one individual in particular who demonstrated a great deal of faith and trust in God. His faith and trust led to his obedience. In Hebrew, God's call on Abraham's life began with "*lech lecha*," which means "Go to yourself!" God commanded Abraham to embark on both a physical and spiritual journey of faith and transformation. Only by leaving his home country would Abraham's true identity be revealed. Like the disciples in John 6, if Abraham believed and obeyed, God would bless him, and he would experience a miracle.

We can't overlook the fact that Abraham was a man of incredible faith and trust. He didn't know where God was sending him, yet, in faith and trust, he went where God directed. Similarly, Yeshua tested His disciples so they would learn to have faith, trust, and obey their calling. In Matthew 28, Yeshua tells them to "go," *lech lecha*, and they did. All of us likewise need to *lech lecha*—"go!"—when God calls. In this way, we can overcome our past baggage, inherited habits, and spiritual limitations, and become all that God has created us to be.

READ | Genesis 12:1–5; Exodus 16:13–23; Deuteronomy 8:1–2; and John 6:1–7

REFLECT

1. Abraham's journey involved testing and struggle that refined his faith and led to him receiving and stewarding the promised blessing. In what ways has God refined your faith? What were some of the challenges that needed faith, trust, and obedience?

2. Put yourselves in the shoes of the Children of Israel for a moment. God instructed them to gather just the manna they needed for the day—and no more. How did the people fare on this test? What would you have thought about the "double portion" instruction after witnessing what happened when the people took too much on other days?

3. According to Deuteronomy 8:1–2, what was the purpose of God testing the Children of Israel in the wilderness? What did God instruct them "to take care" to do?

4. In what ways did Philip's response in John 6:7 limit God's provision and solution? What are some ways that people often try to limit God by finding their own solutions?

5. Yeshua didn't rebuke Philip for his response and his doubts. Instead, He used it show Philip that he could trust in God for provision. We all have times of questions, wrestling, and doubts like Philip, but God doesn't forsake us or condemn us for those feelings. How does it help you to know that God allows *you* to question and wrestle just as Philip—and likely the other eleven disciples—did in this story?

THE EYES HAVE IT

In the teaching for this week, you looked at the story of the blind man whom Yeshua healed in a rather unconventional way. This blind man's eyes were blocked from seeing the world around him. While we examined several aspects of this healing miracle in the group time, let's focus on the importance of sight and how seeing leads to multiplication.

In Hebrew, the word for eyes is *ayin*. We have two eyes. In Jewish thought, symbolically, our two eyes represent actions or choices of the will. One eye is known as the good eye, and one is known as the bad eye. (Yeshua spoke about this in Matthew 6:22–23). The bad eye is the pessimistic and cynical eye. It is always the eye that lets us see the cloud instead of the silver lining. To the degree that we see through the bad eye, we will remain confined and miss breakthroughs and opportunities. However, when we view life through the good eye, we will see blessing, abundant and hopeful life, and good in all people, circumstances, and situations.

An excellent example of seeing through good and bad eyes is found in the story of Moses sending the twelve spies into the Promised Land (see Numbers 13–14). Two of the spies, Joshua and Caleb, could see the good in the land. But the other ten spies could see only the bad. Those ten allowed their bad eyes to prevail, and they returned to Israel's camp speaking about everything wrong with the Promised Land. They said, "The land is good. It flows with milk and honey. It's amazing. Look at the enormous fruit we carried back. It was excellent, *but . . .*"

The ten spies allowed fear to keep them from living the life that God intended to give them. They were afraid of the giants and fortified cities. Their lousy eyesight led to wrong thinking, which led to negative speaking, which undermined the Children of Israel's faith, which caused that generation of Israelites to wander in the desert for forty years—where they died. Their bad eyes caused them to bad-mouth the Promised Land, God, and His promises.

READ | Numbers 13:25–33; Numbers 14:1–12; and John 9:11–16

REFLECT

1. Big "buts" will always get you into trouble. Why do we, like the Israelites and Pharisees, often want to insert our big "buts" into God's plans for us?

[Moses] sent twelve spies to the Promised Land two years after they left Egypt. The people refused to obey God and enter the land because ten of the twelve spies reported that it was too dangerous to enter because of the giants there. Except for Joshua and Caleb, that generation died in the wilderness because of their unwillingness to trust God. The Israelites could have arrived at the Promised Land in two years, but they spent 38 years in the wilderness because of their unbelief.[22]

2. All the spies who went to investigate the land of Canaan saw the same things. However, ten of the spies looked at the situation through "bad eyes" and saw only obstacles that were insurmountable. How did the Children of Israel react to their report? How did God respond when He saw they were not willing to see the situation through a "good eye"?

3. The two spies who gave a favorable report—Joshua and Caleb—had a different spirit. They looked at the obstacles in the Promised Land through hope-filled, faith-filled "good eyes." They were able to see what God wanted to do in this situation because they had their eyes on God. What does it mean to keep our eyes focused on God in this way? How does this different spirit and focus lead to multiplication and renewed sight?

4. Are you more prone to see the "cloud" and never the "silver lining"? Explain your response.

Look what happened to the Children of Israel. They were slaves for hundreds of years. Millions of Israelites saw miracle after miracle—ten plagues in Egypt, the parting of the Red Sea, leaving with the wealth of Egypt, a supernatural provision in the wilderness, hearing the voice of God, seeing the fire, hearing the thunder, experiencing the greatest public revelation of God in history at Mount Sinai. And what did they do? They made a golden calf because Moses took too long to come down from the mountain (see Exodus 32). They lacked faith and trust because of all the generations of hope deferred. They couldn't move completely from hopelessness to healing because they had a slave mentality that they acquired in Egypt.[23]

5. The Children of Israel were not willing to put their faith in God into action and enter the Promised Land. Many believers today act the same—they have faith, but they don't have trust, which is faith in action. In what areas of your life do you need to put faith in God into action instead of continuing to see things through the bad eye?

THE BREAD OF REDEMPTION

In the group time, you discussed the importance of bread (*lechem* in Hebrew). Bread, in some form, is a staple of many cultures' diets, and it has a unique place in Judaism as a physical object of sustenance and spiritual importance. The Jewish people celebrate the Passover, and one aspect is eating *matzah*, unleavened bread. As you saw in this week's teaching, *matzah* symbolizes two things—the bread of affliction and redemption.

Matzah has almost a corrugated look, with holes like dotted lines running vertically alongside rows of browned dough pockets, forming peaks and valleys. The bread represents the centuries of Egypt's enslavement that the Hebrews endured. The brown stripes running the length of the bread recall the lashings of the slave drivers upon the enslaved Jews.

Yeshua is also found in the *matzah*. Yeshua's bread of affliction was the weight of our sins. The *matzah*'s holes stand for His piercings, and the brown stripes represent His stripes by which we are healed and set free from bondage to sin. These personal prisons confine and limit us from being who God wants us to be and doing what He has destined for us—living an abundant life as God takes what we have and multiplies it under His strength, will, and Spirit.

The fourth step in the Passover meal (*seder* in Hebrew) is *yachatz*, which actually means "to break." At this point in the meal, the *matzah* is broken. But even before the Passover meal begins, three pieces of *matzah* are placed in a three-tiered pouch (*matzah tosh*). The leader takes the middle piece and breaks it into two uneven pieces. This middle piece relates to Isaac, the second patriarch, who was bound upon the altar at Moriah, where the Temple would ultimately be built (see Genesis 22). The sacrifice of Isaac foreshadowed and pointed to the death of another Son—the Messiah, the Son of God. The two parts thus refer to the two aspects of the Messiah: Son of Joseph (the suffering Son), and Son of David (the victorious Son).

Bread is critical in the biblical narrative. In this case, the bread/*matzah* lead us to think about Yeshua and how He was afflicted and "broken" for us so that He could redeem us from our sins. By so doing, He gave us eternal and abundant life. When we focus on that truth, we have a mind of breakthrough and multiplication instead of slavery and confinement.

READD | Isaiah 53:4–5; Matthew 26:26; and 1 Corinthians 11:17–34

REFLECT

1. We sometimes view the Last Supper as Yeshua and His disciples sitting around a table eating white bread (thanks to Leonardo DaVinci). How does this background on Passover and *matzah* help you to better understand the details of Holy Communion?

2. Why do you think it is important for Jewish people to annually remember the details of their enslavement in Egypt? Why is it critical for followers of Yeshua to continually remember that "He has borne our griefs and carried our pains" (Isaiah 53:4)?

> *Matzah* symbolizes two things. First, it symbolizes the bread of affliction—*Ha Lachma Anya*. It reminds us of the tasteless bread that our ancestors ate in Egypt, and the slavery they endured. Second, it is also the bread of redemption. When the time of redemption came, God brought the Israelites out of Egypt in such haste that even their bread would not have time to rise. So, they ate unleavened bread—God transformed the symbol of enslavement into the sign and taste of redemption. The bread of affliction and the bread of redemption also point to the comings of the Messiah. In the first coming, He came to suffer—He ate the bread of affliction for us. However, when He returns, we will fully taste the bread of redemption.[24]

3. It's sometimes difficult to recognize that Yeshua came to suffer. Why was it important for Him to suffer? How do His sufferings lead us to a life of multiplication?

4. Yeshua can transform enslavement—addictions, sins, past baggage—into redemption. How can this transformation lead to multiplication?

It's interesting to note that the same Hebrew root for the word *bread* (*lechem*) is also the verb that means "to make war." The Hebrew words have the same letters, which is noteworthy because people war over bread, provision, sustenance, and finances. In the messianic Kingdom, the Messiah will bring abundance and blessing. He will feed everyone without toil and hardship. He will bring *shalom*—peace.[25]

5. "The chastisement for our *shalom* was upon [Yeshua], and by His stripes we are healed" (Isaiah 53:5). How does knowing that the Messiah suffered on your behalf to bring you redemption give you peace (*shalom*)? How have you witnessed God's peace in your life?

CONNECT AND DISCUSS

Take some time today to connect with a group member and discuss some insights from this session. Use any of the prompts below to guide your discussion.

1. What are some of the truths you learned from this study as to why God tests us?

2. How did this session give you new insights into the story of the five loaves and two fish?

3. In this session, we talked about both faith and trust. In what one area of your life do you need to more actively trust God for His provision?

CATCH UP AND READ AHEAD

Use this time to go back and complete any study and reflection questions from previous days this week that you weren't able to finish. Make a note below of any revelations you've had and reflect on any growth or personal insights you've gained.

Read chapters 9–10 in *Signs and Secrets of the Messiah* before the next group session. Use the space below to make note of anything that stands out to you or encourages you from your reading.

WEEK 5

BEFORE GROUP MEETING	Read chapters 9-10 in *Signs and Secrets of the Messiah* Read the Welcome section (page 83)
GROUP MEETING	Discuss the Connect questions Watch the video teaching for session 5 Discuss the questions that follow as a group Do the closing exercise and pray (pages 83–88)
STUDY 1	Complete the personal study (pages 90–92)
STUDY 2	Complete the personal study (pages 93–94)
STUDY 3	Complete the personal study (pages 95–97)
CONNECT AND DISCUSS	Connect with someone in your group (page 98)
WRAP IT UP	Complete any unfinished personal studies Connect with your group about the next study that you want to go through together

THE SIGNS AND SECRETS OF FULLNESS

"Amen, amen I tell you, he who puts his trust in Me, the works that I do he will do; and greater than these he will do, because I am going to the Father."

JOHN 14:12

We have covered a lot of territory of this study. We have seen how Yeshua's signs and miracles have changed lives, healed people, infuriated religious leaders, and set Him apart as the greater than Moses. Through the apostle John's eyes, we've uncovered signs and miracles of transformation and purification, new birth, healing and wholeness, and multiplication.

We've also seen Yeshua serve people in need with each sign or miracle that He performed during His ministry on earth. We've seen Him refute the religious leaders, even as they tried to trap Him into the Law versus His grace. We've also witnessed incredible signs that revealed His identity and gave the disciples an example of their future.

Now, as we come to this final session in *Signs and Secrets of the Messiah*, we will look at one last miracle that Yeshua performed after His death and resurrection. This miracle takes place in John 21, the last chapter in that Gospel, where Yeshua instructed His disciples to fish from the right side of the boat—leading to a miraculous catch of 153 fish. We will examine the significance of the "right side," the number 153, and revisit a concept from our last session—faith and trust.

In this last session, we will also examine *our* opportunity to serve others miraculously. We will look at the inheritance that Yeshua left to the disciples—and to us—when He ascended into heaven. While some feared His leaving, the gospel is clear that we should not be afraid but act out of the boldness with which He left us. It's an exciting prospect!

CONNECT | 15 MINUTES

Get the session started by choosing one of these questions to discuss as a group:

- What was something that spoke to your heart from last week's personal study that you would like to share with the group?

  — *or* —

- When is a time you did something unsuccessful on your own but found God had another way for you—and it turned out even better than you imagined?

WATCH | 20 MINUTES

Now watch the video for this session. Below is an outline of the key points covered during the teaching. Record any key concepts that stand out to you.

OUTLINE

   I. Peter and a few disciples went fishing after Yeshua's resurrection (see John 21:1–14).

      A. The disciples fished all night but caught nothing.

      B. Yeshua, from the beach, told the disciples to cast their nets again.

      C. This time, their nets were full almost to breaking.

  II. The Hebrew word for fish (*dag*) also means anxiety or fear.

      A. God doesn't want us to be anxious or worried about what may or may not happen to us.

      B. Fear undermines faith and corrupts our vision. It causes us to believe in the worst possible future imaginable. Fear leads to pessimism and cynicism.

      C. Faith empowers, propels, and gives us momentum. Faith helps us to overcome.

 III. There are hidden secrets and meaning in the number 153.

      A. The number 153 points to Yeshua as the divine messianic King.

      B. The number 153 points to the Passover Lamb.

      C. The number 153 points to the Torah and the richness of reading and studying God's Word.

 IV. The "right side" connects to the Torah as well as God's fullness.

      A. The right side is associated with *chesed*, God's lovingkindness.

      B. We must be aware of which side we are fishing from—not from the side of judgment but from the side of God's Word and lovingkindness—to see the great catch of fish come in our lives.

  V. Yeshua taught with power and authority and grants the same to each of us (see John 14:12).

      A. Yeshua emptied Himself of His divinity (see Philippians 2:7–8). He performed His miracles out of His humanity, not out of His divinity.

      B. Yeshua promised the disciples that they would receive power as well as authority when the Holy Spirit came upon them at Pentecost (see Matthew 28:18–19; Acts 1:8).

      C. The purpose of God giving us power and authority is to fulfill His initial calling at Mount Sinai for us to be a holy priesthood and a royal nation that impacts the world.

NOTES

DISCUSS | 35 MINUTES

Now discuss what you just watched by answering the following questions.

1. It was a challenging time for the disciple Peter. He had denied the Lord three times, yet he saw the empty tomb and knew Yeshua had risen from the grave. Now he was fishing, and Yeshua was standing on the beach. What thoughts do you think went through Peter's mind as he wondered if he still had a role to play in the new Yeshua movement?

2. Ask someone in the group to read aloud Psalm 38:18. Peter had anxiety and fear because he was troubled by what he had done. What is your definition of *fear* and *anxiety*? How can fear get a grip on us and undermine our faith in Yeshua?

3. How has God provided fullness for you when you have obeyed His specific instructions for your life?

4. Ask someone in the group to read aloud John 14:12–14. Does it surprise you that you have the *same* power and authority as Jesus? Why or why not? Do you have examples of how you've used the power and authority Yeshua has given to you?

5. Yeshua said, "My sheep hear My voice. I know them, and they follow Me" (John 10:27). How does our inability to hear our Shepherd's voice hinder our healing, power, and authority? What specifically do you do to tune into His voice?

RESPOND | 10 MINUTES

As you close this session, take a few minutes to write down three key ideas that you will remember from this study. When everyone is finished, share your responses with the group.

1.

2.

3.

PRAY | 10 MINUTES

End your time by praying together. As you pray, ask the Lord to reveal any areas where you are fishing from the right side of the boat. Ask Him to fill you with His power and authority to do what He has called you to do. Finally, write down any prayer requests in the space below so that you and your group members can continue to pray about them in the weeks ahead.

Name   **Request**

PERSONAL STUDY

As you learned this week, Peter and several other disciples returned to fishing on the Sea of Galilee after Yeshua's resurrection. It was there that Yeshua met them and performed a miracle that revealed He still had plans for them. In the personal studies for this week, you will go deeper into this miracle and explore several other concepts about the fullness that God provides. As you work through each day's study, write down your responses to the questions. If you are reading *Signs and Secrets of the Messiah*, first review chapters 9 and 10 in the book.

RETURNING TO A PLACE OF FAMILIARITY

One of the primary characters in John 21 is the apostle Peter. He was now at a point of confusion. Remember, Peter had denied Yeshua three times at the crucifixion. But then, after the women found Yeshua's tomb empty and ran back to camp, Peter and John went to investigate for themselves and also found it empty. What confusion must have coursed through Peter's mind! He would remember Yeshua telling him that "on this rock I will build my church" (Matthew 16:18 NIV), but he probably had doubts that he could ever be *that* person again.

So what did he do? He returned to a place of familiarity. Remember what Peter was doing when Jesus first met him? *Fishing.* Now, at the end of John's Gospel, we find him and a few others out fishing again. As pastor R. Kent Hughes wrote, "As usual, Peter's inability to sit still helped create that stage. The aroma of the sea and the addictive rhythm of lapping water were too much for Peter. Finally, he blurted out to his companions, 'I'm going out to fish' (John 21:3). The other disciples immediately voiced their approval."[26]

Before we criticize Peter—and ask why he wasn't out preaching about the resurrection instead of going fishing—we need to consider what it means to return to a familiar place. Familiarity is comfortable. It produces automatic or learned responses that cause us to use less energy. Familiarity gives us a feeling of stability. This was much needed in Peter's case. It is likely that he, at least, went fishing out of *fear*. He was fearful of this future, and this caused him great anxiety. So he went to a familiar place, seeking comfort, rest, and stability. But what happened? Peter and the other seasoned fishermen caught *nothing*. Their nets were empty. This probably caused them more anxiety. Not only did they not know about their future, but they also couldn't be successful at what they *did* know—their trade as fishermen.

Fear and anxiety have no place in a believer's mind. God doesn't want us to be anxious or worried about what may or may not happen. He wants us to instead live in His fullness so we move away from fear, worry, and anxiety to faith. Then, as we believe, we move from faith to trust that God will show up. He showed up for Peter, and He will show up for us as well.

READ | John 21:1-11; Philippians 4:4-7; and Hebrews 11:1

REFLECT

1. The apostle Paul writes that we are not to be "anxious about anything" (Philippians 4:6). What things tend to trouble you and cause you the most worry and anxiety? Can you contrast how the world deals with anxiety with how God wants you to handle it?

> Peter had denied the Lord. He probably thought there was no longer a major role for him and certainly not as the leader or rock of this new Yeshua-Jesus movement. He returned to a place of familiarity. Maybe you've heard this old saying: *When the going gets tough, the tough go fishing.* . . . Peter and the disciples were fishing from a place of anxiety and worry about their future. God doesn't want you to be anxious or worried about what may or may not happen to you.[27]

2. We must understand that fear is false faith. True faith believes the best, while fear thinks the worst. Fear only serves to undermine faith and corrupts our vision. Looking at the study, how was Peter's fear an example of false faith? Think of an example of false faith in your own life. How did God turn it around to genuine faith and trust?

3. How would you define true faith? What does it believe? How does your definition match up with the definition of faith given in Hebrews 11:1?

4. The disciples went to a place of familiarity. Why do we often return to those places, even if it means enslavement to old habits and harmful patterns?

> If you want your nets to be full, you must operate out of a place of faith, not fear, worry, and anxiety. When you stay in fear, your net is always going to be empty. When you live in faith, the miraculous comes into your life, and your net becomes full.[28]

5. How do we move from fear to faith? How can we set anxiety aside and trust the Lord?

WHY 153 FISH?

In this week's group time, you learned some of the meanings behind the number of fish the disciples caught. They brought in 153 fish. This seems like an odd number. Why 153? As you learned in the teaching, the number 153 points to Messiah's identity. You also saw that 153 confirms Yeshua as the divine messianic King and Passover Lamb. But there's more.

The number 153 also connects to the Passover Lamb, as pointed out in the teaching, and something else related to Passover. Exodus 12:11 tells us that the Israelites were to eat the first Passover "in haste" (bə·ḥip·pā·zō·wn in Hebrew). "In haste" equals 153. This verse and the Hebrew phrase thus teach us that we need to eagerly wait for redemption with a life that eagerly anticipates the Messiah's return. We should long to come out of Egypt's bondage and confinement and live in a state of expectation and readiness for Him. This sense of anticipation was also how the disciples were to live and fish! There is a sense of urgency.

The number 153 points to not only Yeshua's identity but ours as well. The Hebrew phrase *Bnei HaElohim*, or "children of God," equals 153. So does the phrase, in Greek, "sprinkled clean," as found in Hebrews 10:22. Other expressions that equal 153 are "heirs" (*klēronomous* in Greek) and "inherit" (*yan-ḥi-len-nāh* in Hebrew). So Yeshua, the Lord of Glory (153) and Passover Lamb (153), gave His life so that all who believe become children of God (153) and are sprinkled clean (153), unifying Gentile and Jew to be one people (153), becoming heirs (153) whom He will cause to inherit (153) eternal life in the Kingdom of God!

Finally, Yeshua's first miracle (turning water into wine) connects to His last (the fullness of the nets). The phrase "days are coming soon" in Hebrew equals 153. Amos 9:13 speaks of the plowman overtaking the reaper and the mountains dripping with sweet wine. This verse in Amos speaks to fullness, just as the servants filled the six water pots in Yeshua's first miracle to the brim. Also, near the middle of Yeshua's ministry, He showed fullness with five loaves, two fish, and leftovers in the baskets. Then, in John 21, the nets overflowed with similar abundance and fullness. Yeshua is thus showing fullness from the beginning of His ministry to the end—and the days are coming when we will experience the fullness of Yeshua for all eternity.

READ | Exodus 12:11; Amos 9:13; John 1:10–12; Romans 8:17; and 1 John 3:1–10

REFLECT

1. What does Exodus 12:11 indicate about how God wanted His people to be ready for their redemption from the Egyptians? How does this apply to our lives today?

2. How does Amos 9:13 speak to God's promise of fullness in our lives?

3. God holds you "by your right hand" like a father leading a child. In fact, the apostle John uses the phrase "children of God" in his first epistle to describe Yeshua's followers (1 John 3:1 NIV). Besides equaling 153, it's a term of endearment. What does it mean to you to be a child of God? What does it mean to have your identity in Yeshua Messiah?

4. In Romans 8:17, Paul writes that we are "heirs of God and joint-heirs with Messiah." What do you think about when you read the phrase "heirs of God"? What sort of inheritance are you expecting from the Lord?

> We've been studying the miracles and mysteries found in the book of John. The reason for these signs and wonders was to demonstrate that He, Yeshua, was and is the promised messianic King. . . . From beginning to end, John tries to show Yeshua as the promised messianic King of Israel, and the number 153 supports that. Because who is the King of glory? 153. It is Yeshua.[29]

5. Most of the words and phrases connected to 153 carry with them the thought of fullness or abundance. Which of the phrases stand out to you? Why?

TURNING ON THE POWER

Yeshua taught with power and authority. He operated in a way that resulted in miracles. His power, authority, and miracles demonstrated the proof of His message. This set Yeshua apart from others, because Yeshua wasn't the only one who performed miracles. These three attributes sparked jealousy in the self-righteous teachers and among some rabbis.

Yeshua granted that same power and authority to His disciples. The good news is that when we are born again, Yeshua gives us the same power and authority. Some think the miracles were only for Yeshua and the apostles, and that period has ended. But many people have witnessed miracles today. Yeshua said in John 14:12 that we could do works that are not only like His but potentially even greater than the ones He did. Those words may seem impossible. How can we possibly do miracles on the level of Yeshua or some that are even more remarkable? We must operate out of the power and direction of the Holy Spirit.

To experience fullness, we can't operate in our strength, wisdom, or will. We can't merely ask God to bless what we do. The only way for our net to be full of divine favor and blessings is by operating in the power of the *Ruach*—the power of the Spirit. The Holy Spirit sows God's Word into our lives. He is our comforter, healer, intercessor, and spiritual advisor. We need to always listen to the voice of the Holy Spirit.

When the disciples cast the nets a second time, they were empowered. When they went out after Yeshua's ascension and spoke with authority, they spoke under the power of the Holy Spirit. Their nets were full—they saw God's fullness as people came to know Yeshua. All aspects of a full life are covered by the power and authority given to us through the power of the Holy Spirit. The power of the Holy Spirit will help us experience overflowing nets and a great catch.

READ | Isaiah 11:2; John 15:1–5; and Acts 1:8

REFLECT

1. God wants you to have victories as the Holy Spirit works through you. When is a time that you witnessed the Holy Spirit's power at work through your life?

2. You have been given the same power and authority as Yeshua Messiah. In what ways does knowing that help you overcome any fear to do what God is calling you to do?

We need to operate in the *Ruach* to see the abundance in our lives. Sometimes we've caught nothing, or we're experiencing lack, because we're not operating according to God's plan, wisdom, and power. We need our nets strengthened by continually relying upon the power of the Spirit. Here's what may help you—take time to pray and ask the Holy Spirit to guide you in all aspects of your life.[30]

3. Often, we come up with great ideas for our next move in life. We ask God to bless those ideas without taking the time to pray and ask what His plans and intentions are for us. What does Yeshua say about abiding in Him in John 15:1-5? How does abiding in Him help us to know when we are moving ahead of His plans for our lives?

It's not *great* ideas that we need but *God* ideas implemented in the power of the Spirit that will help us experience the great catch. This is the point of John 15:5: "I am the vine and you are the branches. Those who stay *united* with me, and I with them, are the ones who bear much fruit; because apart from me *you can't do a thing*" (CJB, emphasis mine). In Greek, do you know what the word *thing* means? It means "nothing." In Hebrew, *efes* means nothing, zilch, zero. And in Yiddish, such a colorful language, the phrase is *gornisht mit gornisht*, which means, "a whole lot of nothing."[31]

4. Yeshua said to His disciples, "Every branch in Me that does not bear fruit, He takes away; and every branch that bears fruit, He trims so that it may bear more fruit" (John 15:2). How have you witnessed this "trimming" process in your life?

5. Yeshua promised that you would "receive power when the Holy Spirit comes on you" (Acts 1:8 NIV). The Holy Spirit will guide you through the maze of life much like an air traffic controller. The controller assumes that the pilot understands the flight manual. Such is the case with the Holy Spirit. How is the Holy Spirit's guidance blocked if you don't know God's Word? What are some ways the Holy Spirit can lead you to better understand God's Word and provide you with His power and authority?

CONNECT AND DISCUSS

Take some time today to connect with a group member and discuss some insights from this session. Use any of the prompts below to guide your discussion.

1. What is one of the most life-changing things you learned during this study?

2. How does knowing that Jesus wants you to have a life of fullness help you to know and trust Him more—especially during challenging times?

3. How has this study helped you recognize that returning to the familiar isn't always the best option that will lead to "nets that are full"?

WRAP IT UP

Use this time to go back and complete any of the study and reflection questions from previous days that you weren't able to finish. Make a note below of any questions you've had and reflect on any growth or personal insights you've gained. Finally, discuss with your group what studies you might want to go through next and when you will plan on meeting together again.

LEADER'S GUIDE

Thank you for your willingness to lead your group through this study! What you have chosen to do is valuable and will make a great difference in the lives of others. *Signs and Secrets of the Messiah* is a five-session Bible study built around video content and small-group interaction. As the group leader, imagine yourself as the host of a party. Your job is to take care of your guests by managing the details so that when your guests arrive, they can focus on one another and on the interaction around the topic for that session.

Your role as the group leader is not to answer all the questions or reteach the content—the video, book, and study guide will do most of that work. Your job is to guide the experience and cultivate your small group into a connected and engaged community. This will make it a place for members to process, question, and reflect—not necessarily receive more instruction.

There are several elements in this leader's guide that will help you as you structure your study and reflection time, so be sure to follow along and take advantage of each one.

BEFORE YOU BEGIN

Before your first meeting, make sure the group members have a copy of this study guide. Alternatively, you can hand out the study guides at your first meeting and give the members some time to look over the material and ask any preliminary questions. Also make sure they are aware that they have access to the streaming videos at any time. During your first meeting, ask the members to provide their name, phone number, and email address so you can keep in touch with them.

Generally, the ideal size for a group is eight to ten people, which will ensure that everyone has enough time to participate in discussions. If you have more people, you might want to break up the main group into smaller subgroups. Encourage those who show up at the first meeting to commit to attending the meetings for the duration of the study, as this will help the group members get to know one another, create stability for the group, and help you know how to best prepare to lead them through the material.

Each of the sessions begins with an opening reflection in the Welcome section. The questions that follow in the Connect section serve as an icebreaker to get the group members thinking about the topic. Some people may want to tell a long story in response to one of these questions, but the goal is to keep the answers brief. Ideally, you want everyone in the group to get a chance to answer, so try to keep the responses to a minute or less. If you have talkative group members, say up front that everyone needs to limit their answer to one minute.

Give the group members a chance to answer, but also tell them to feel free to pass if they wish. With the rest of the study, it's generally not a good idea to have everyone answer every question—a free-flowing discussion is more desirable. But with the opening icebreaker questions, you can go around the circle. Encourage shy people to share, but don't force them.

At your first meeting, let the group members know that each session contains a personal study section they can use to continue to engage with the content until the next meeting. While this is optional, it will help them cement the concepts presented during the group study time and help them better understand the signs and secrets of the Messiah. Let them know that if they choose to do so, they can watch the video for the next session by accessing the streaming code. Invite them to bring any questions and insights to your next meeting, especially if they had a breakthrough moment or didn't understand something.

PREPARATION FOR EACH SESSION

As the leader, there are a few things you should do to prepare for each meeting:

- **Read through the session.** This will help you become more familiar with the content and know how to structure the discussion times.

- **Decide how the videos will be used.** Determine whether you want the members to watch the videos ahead of time (again, via the streaming access code) or together as a group.

- **Decide which questions you want to discuss.** Based on the length of your group discussions, you may not be able to get through all the questions. So look over the questions in each session and choose which ones you definitely want to cover.

- **Be familiar with the questions you want to discuss.** When the group meets, you'll be watching the clock, so make sure you are familiar with the questions that you have selected. In this way, you will ensure that you have the material more deeply in your mind than your group members.

- **Pray for your group.** Pray for your group members and ask God to lead them as they study His Word.

In many cases, there will be no one "right" answer to the question. Answers will vary, especially when the group members are being asked to share their personal experiences.

STRUCTURING THE DISCUSSION TIME

You will need to determine with your group how long you want to meet so you can plan your time accordingly. Suggested times for each section have been provided in this study guide, and if you adhere to these times, your group will meet for ninety minutes, as noted below. If you want to meet for two hours, follow the times given in the right-hand column:

Section	90 Minutes	120 Minutes
CONNECT (discuss one or more of the opening questions for the session)	15 minutes	20 minutes
WATCH (watch the teaching material together and take notes)	20 minutes	20 minutes
DISCUSS (discuss the study questions you selected ahead of time)	35 minutes	50 minutes
RESPOND (write down key takeaways)	10 minutes	15 minutes
PRAY (pray together and dismiss)	10 minutes	15 minutes

As the group leader, it is up to you to keep track of the time and keep things on schedule. You might want to set a timer for each segment so both you and the group members know when your time is up. Don't be concerned if the group members are quiet or slow to share. People are often quiet when they are pulling together their ideas, and this might be a new experience for them. Just ask a question and then let it hang in the air for a while until someone shares. You can then say, "Thank you. What about others? What came to you when you watched that portion of the teaching?"

GROUP DYNAMICS

Leading a group through *Signs and Secrets of the Messiah* will prove to be highly rewarding both to you and your group members. But you still may encounter challenges along the way! Discussions can get off track. Group members may not be sensitive to the needs and ideas of others. Some might worry they will be expected to talk about matters that make them feel awkward. Others may express comments that result in disagreements. To help ease this strain on you and the group, consider the following ground rules:

- When someone raises a question or comment that is off the main topic, suggest that you deal with it another time, or, if you feel led to go in that direction, let the group know you will be spending some time discussing it.

- If someone asks a question that you don't know how to answer, admit it and move on. At your discretion, feel free to invite group members to comment on questions that call for personal experience.

- If you find one or two people are dominating the discussion time, direct a few questions to others in the group. Outside the main group time, ask the more dominating members to help you draw out the quieter ones. Work to make them a part of the solution instead of part of the problem.

- When a disagreement occurs, encourage the group members to process the matter in love. Encourage those on opposite sides to restate what they heard the other side say about the matter, and then invite each side to evaluate if that perception is accurate. Lead the group in examining other scriptures related to the topic and look for common ground.

When any of these issues arise, encourage your group members to follow these words from Scripture: "Love one another" (John 13:34); "If possible, so far as it depends on you, live in *shalom* with all people" (Romans 12:18); and "Be quick to listen, slow to speak, and slow to anger" (James 1:19).

Thank you again for taking the time to lead your group. You are making a difference in your group members' lives and having an impact as they learn about the signs and secrets of the Messiah in the Gospel of John.

ABOUT THE AUTHOR

Rabbi Jason Sobel is the founder of Fusion Global, a ministry that seeks to bring people into the full inheritance of the faith by connecting treasures of "the old and the new." Rabbi Jason's voice is authentic, being raised in a Jewish home, and qualified by years of diligent academic work. He received his rabbinic ordination from the UMJC (Union of Messianic Jewish Congregations) in 2005, has a BA in Jewish Studies (Moody), and has an MA in Intercultural Studies (Southeastern Seminary). He is a sought-after speaker and the author of *Breakthrough; Aligning with God's Appointed Times*; *Mysteries of the Messiah*; and *Signs and Secrets of the Messiah*. He is also the coauthor, with Kathie Lee Gifford, of the *New York Times* bestseller *The Rock, the Road, and the Rabbi* and of *The God of the Way*.

ENDNOTES

1. Kerry and Chris Shook, *Find Your Miracle: How the Miracles of Jesus Can Change Your Life Today* (New York: WaterBrook, 2016), 3.
2. Brant Pitre, *Jesus the Bridegroom: The Greatest Love Story Ever Told* (New York: Image, 2014), 41.
3. Rabbi Jason Sobel, *Signs and Secrets of the Messiah: A Fresh Look at the Miracles of Jesus* (Nashville, TN: W Publishing Group, 2023), 20.
4. Sobel, *Signs and Secrets of the Messiah*, 24.
5. *The William Davidson Talmud* (Korean—Steinsaltz), Berakhot 34b, https://www.sefaria.org/Berakhot.34b.24?ven=William_Davidson_Edition_-_English&vhe=William_Davidson_Edition_-_Vocalized_Aramaic&lang=bi&with=all&lang2=en.
6. Sobel, *Signs and Secrets of the Messiah*, 19.
7. Sobel, *Signs and Secrets of the Messiah*, 20.
8. *Thayer's Greek Definitions* published in 1886, 1889, public domain.
9. Charles R. Swindoll, *Swindoll's Living Insights New Testament Commentary: Matthew 16–28* (Carol Stream, IL: Tyndale House Publishers, Inc., 2020), 152.
10. Sobel, *Signs and Secrets of the Messiah*, 55–56.
11. Sobel, *Signs and Secrets of the Messiah*, 86.
12. Warren W. Wiersbe, *Be Counted*, "Be" Commentary Series (Colorado Springs, CO: Chariot Victor Pub., 1999), 92.
13. Sobel, *Signs and Secrets of the Messiah*, 65.
14. Sobel, *Signs and Secrets of the Messiah*, 67.
15. Sobel, *Signs and Secrets of the Messiah*, 66–67.
16. Hal Lindsey, cited in Denise Lorenz, *Be Free From Fear: Overcoming Fear to Live Free* (Life Changer Press, 2013), eBook edition.
17. Sobel, *Signs and Secrets of the Messiah*, 78–79.
18. Sobel, *Signs and Secrets of the Messiah*, 90.
19. Sobel, *Signs and Secrets of the Messiah*, xv.
20. Sobel, *Signs and Secrets of the Messiah*, 82–83.
21. Sobel, *Signs and Secrets of the Messiah*, 83.
22. Sobel, *Signs and Secrets of the Messiah*, 66–67.
23. Sobel, *Signs and Secrets of the Messiah*, 82.
24. Sobel, *Signs and Secrets of the Messiah*, 88–89.
25. Sobel, *Signs and Secrets of the Messiah*, 148–149.
26. Sobel, *Signs and Secrets of the Messiah*, 152.
27. R. Kent Hughes, *John: That You May Believe*, Preaching the Word Commentary Series (Wheaton, IL: Crossway Books, 1999), 462.
28. Sobel, *Signs and Secrets of the Messiah*, 196.
29. Sobel, *Signs and Secrets of the Messiah*, 197.
30. Sobel, *Signs and Secrets of the Messiah*, 203.
31. Sobel, *Signs and Secrets of the Messiah*, 197–198.
32. Sobel, *Signs and Secrets of the Messiah*, 198.

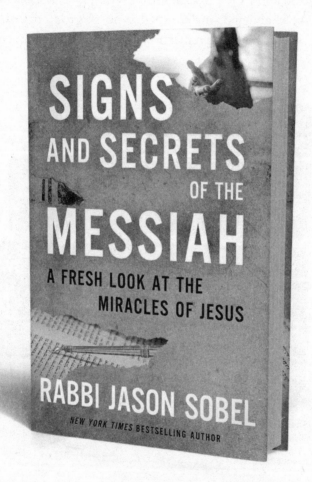

Also Available

In this six-session video Bible study, Kathie Lee Gifford and Rabbi Jason Sobel helps you apply the principles in *The Rock, the Road, and the Rabbi* to your life. The study guide includes video notes, group discussion questions, and personal study and reflection materials for in-between sessions.

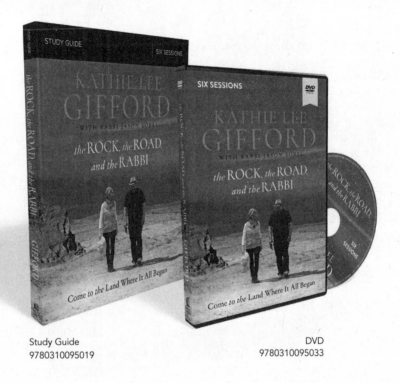

Study Guide
9780310095019

DVD
9780310095033

**Available now at your favorite bookstore,
or streaming video on StudyGateway.com.**

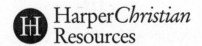

HarperChristian
Resources

ALSO AVAILABLE

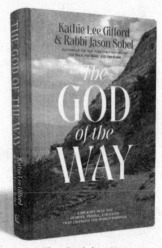

The God the Way
ISBN 9780785290438
On sale September 2022

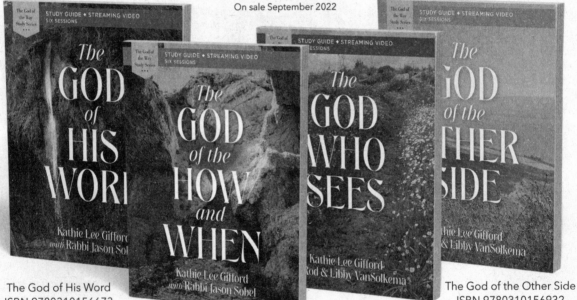

The God of His Word
ISBN 9780310156673
On sale April 2023

The God of the How and When
ISBN 9780310156543
On sale November 2022

The God Who Sees
ISBN 9780310156802
On sale October 2023

The God of the Other Side
ISBN 9780310156932
On sale January 2024

Available wherever books are sold